One

PAT BARKER

PAT BARKER

SHARON MONTEITH

Northcote House
in association with the
British Council

© Copyright 2002 by Sharon Monteith

First published in 2002 by Northcote House Publishers Ltd, Horndon, Tavistock, Devon, PL19 9NQ, United Kingdom.
Tel: +44 (01822) 810066. Fax: +44 (01822) 810034.

British Library Cataloguing-in-Publication Data
A catalogue record for this book is available from the British Library

ISBN 0-7463-0900-7

Typeset by TW Typesetting, Plymouth, Devon
Printed and bound in the United Kingdom by Bell & Bain Ltd., Glasgow

For my mother and my father with love

and for my friends Jenny Newman and
David Evans and Pat and David Wheeler

Contents

Acknowledgements

I would like to thank colleagues and friends: Pat and Dave Wheeler, Jenny Newman and Dave Evans, George Wotton, Dennis Brown, Sue and Tom Weitzel, and Nahem Yousaf. I would also like to thank Pat and David Barker for their hospitality and, in particular, Pat Barker for the precious writing time she gave up to be interviewed at such length. Finally, my thanks go to Brian Hulme and Hilary Walford at Northcote House.

Biographical Outline

1943	Born 8 May in Thornaby-on-Tees. Mother Moyra Drake; brought up mainly by her grandparents.
1954	Attended King James Grammar School, Knaresborough.
1955	Moved to Grangefield Grammar School, Stockton-on-Tees.
1962–5	Read International History at London School of Economics.
1965–6	Diploma of Education, University of Durham.
1966–70	Taught at a number of Further Education Colleges on Teesside.
1969	Partnership with David Barker, Professor of Zoology at University of Durham, begins.
1970	Birth of son, John David.
1974	Birth of daughter, Annabel Elizabeth.
1978	Marries David Barker. Encouraged and influenced by Angela Carter on Lumb Bank writing course.
1982	*Union Street* published by Virago Press. Joint winner of the Fawcett Society Book Prize.
1983	Nominated as one of twenty Best Young British Novelists by the Book Marketing Council.
1984	*Blow Your House Down* published by Virago Press. A Danish translation of *Union Street* is published by Rosinante, the first of many foreign language editions, including translations into Hebrew and Japanese.
1986	*The Century's Daughter* published by Virago Press. *Blow Your House Down* adapted for the stage by Jane

Thomas as *The Chicken Factory*. Performed in Hull by the Company of Women.

1988   *The Man Who Wasn't There* published by Penguin. *Union Street* made into a Hollywood film directed by Martin Ritt, starring Jane Fonda and Robert de Niro. Original title, *Letters*, changed to *Stanley and Iris*. The film bears very little resemblance to the novel.

1990   *Stanley and Iris* released in the US (February) and in the UK (June). Virago Press publish a film tie-in edition. *Union Street* published in Italian as *Lettere D'Amore*.

1991   *Regeneration* published by Penguin, the first of what is to become the Regeneration Trilogy.

1992   *Regeneration* published by Dutton (Penguin, USA) as a William Abrahams book. Chosen as one of the four best novels of the year by the editors of the *New York Times Book Review*.

1993   *The Eye in the Door* published by Viking. Awarded the Guardian Prize for Fiction and won the Special Award category of the Northern Electric Arts Awards. Pat Barker awarded the degree of Hon. M.Litt by the University of Teeside. Contributed to *Writing on the Wall* (published by Weidenfeld & Nicolson) as one of twenty women writers writing about their favourite work of art by a female artist in the Tate Gallery. Barker chose three sculptures by Elizabeth Frink and wrote a piece entitled 'Footprints in the Snow'.

1995   *The Ghost Road* published by Viking. Awarded the Booker Prize for Fiction. *Blow Your House Down* adapted by Sarah Daniels as a play of the same title and performed by Live Theatre in Newcastle and Bishop Auckland.

1996   *Regeneration, The Eye in the Door*, and *The Ghost Road* published by Viking in one volume as *The Regeneration Trilogy*. *Union Street, Blow Your House Down*, and *The Century's Daughter* published by Virago as Modern Classics, *The Century's Daughter* under Barker's original title, *Liza's England*. Awarded Author of the Year Prize by the Booksellers' Association. Awarded the degree of Hon. D.Litt by Napier University, Edinburgh. Featured in BBC2 documentary, *On the Ghost Road*, touring the battlefields of northern France.

1997   *Regeneration* made into a film of the same title directed by Gillie Mackinnon starring Jonathan Pryce (as Rivers), James Wilby (as Sassoon), and Jonny Lee Miller (as Billy Prior). Released in the USA as *Behind the Lines*. Elected Honorary Fellow of the London School of Economics and Political Science. Awarded Hon. Ph.D. by the Open University, and by the University of Hertfordshire.

1998   *Another World* published by Viking.

1999   Awarded CBE in New Year's Honours List.

2001   *Border Crossing* published by Viking.

Abbreviations and References

AI	Author interview: unpublished interview with Pat Barker, conducted by Sharon Monteith and Pat Wheeler, Durham, February 1999
AW	*Another World* (London: Viking, 1998)
BC	*Border Crossing* (London: Viking, 2001)
BYHD	*Blow Your House Down* (London: Virago, 1984)
ED	*The Eye in the Door* (London: Viking, 1993)
GR	*The Ghost Road* (London: Viking 1995)
LE	*Liza's England* (formerly *The Century's Daughter*) (London: Virago, 1996)
MWWT	*The Man Who Wasn't There* (London: Penguin, 1988)
R.	*Regeneration* (London: Penguin, 1991)
UC	*Union Street* (London: Virago, 1982)

For such a successful British writer, translated into many foreign languages, achieving huge worldwide sales and the subject of a number of interviews and articles, Barker has also been subject to some provocatively reductive reviewing. Reviewers have tended to split Barker's œuvre into two distinct periods – 1982 to 1991 and 1991 to the present – reinforced by the belief that her attention to gender shifts dramatically from women to men in these periods. For Annabel Davis-Goff, for example, Barker is 'a modern-day Mrs Gaskell' who writes 'in a different voice' when she embarks on the Trilogy. As soon as *Regeneration* and *The Eye in the Door* were published, Candice Rodd decided, 'You could almost be forgiven for thinking that there are two Pat Barkers – the one who writes gritty contemporary feminist novels set in working-class areas of northern England, and the author of profoundly thoughtful fiction about the devastating psychological damage sustained by soldiers fighting the First World War.' Novelist and *Guardian* reviewer Philip Hensher calls the early fiction 'sociological' and feels that Barker constrained those fictions by 'limiting her subject matter' to working-class and predominantly female communities. He feels she finds her subject in the First World War and that she begins to write 'novels of ideas', not 'anecdotal evocations', as he describes her first novel *Union Street*.[3] I believe that it is erroneous to imply that novels that situate the violence of war are 'about' men and those that feature women in coexistence are exclusively 'about' traditionally 'female' preoccupations. As Barker has reiterated, 'I never thought for a second that feminism is only about women.'[4] Barker is much more energized by the ways in which gender stereotyping may distort and repress the personal development of individuals of both genders. From Kelly Brown in her very first novel, *Union Street*, to Stephen in *Liza's England*, to her best-known and iconoclastic creation Billy Prior, sexuality and sexual ambivalence have underpinned her exploration of relationships. In *Regeneration*, through the military psychiatrist W. H. R. Rivers, she states quite clearly that there are few unequivocal gender boundaries: 'The War that had promised so much in the way of "manly" activity had actually delivered "feminine" passivity, and on a scale that their mothers and sisters had scarcely known' (*R.* 108). Rivers

2

thinks of boyish fantasies of warfare crushed by the reality of war itself: men and boys find themselves scared, paralysed by fear, helplessly waiting in the trenches for death to come and find them instead of being able to fight it.

Her cumulative evaluation of sexuality and psychology has led critics to reassess the fiction and draw Barker into discussions of postmodernism and deconstruction. Labels and labelling are, of course, the signposts critics use to find their way round contemporary fiction, but there exists a familiar reviewing trap of equating postmodernist complexities with 'intellectual' writing – or 'novels of ideas' – and of assuming that fictions that may be described as 'working class' necessarily render their themes in naturalistic, autobiographical, and less theorized ways. This is simply not the case, as critics from Raymond Williams to Peter Hitchcock have shown. Some early reviewers made the mistake in their search for the sociological data *behind* the novels of overlooking their *art*. They also failed to acknowledge that stories of both world wars, and of emotional and physical conflict in general, have long been a source of concern for Barker. In an interview published in the same year as *Regeneration* she equated poor women's communities in post-industrial Britain with the camaraderie of soldiers in the trenches. She notes the same humour and stoicism, 'fighting a war that should not have been fought ... without any idea of what the alternatives are'.[5] One might also add that the 'foul' language sometimes used to express working-class anger and anxiety that readers encounter in *Union Street* and *Blow Your House Down* was first commonly used in the trenches, where the putrefaction and squalor exceeded the men's descriptive powers.

A sense of stoical endurance characterizes each of her novels, at their most gritty and disturbing and at their most lyrical and philosophical, as when in *Liza's England* Barker has Frank ponder on men living their lives by the factory clock: 'Clocking on, clocking off, time anaesthetised, vivisected ... the working class selling the carcase of time' (*LE* 151). Or when Wilfred Owen in *Regeneration* describes the trenches as ancient labyrinths filled with skulls that seem to grow out of the mud like mushrooms (*R.* 84). The resilience and articulateness of the working classes are precisely what draw someone like the socially conscious filmmaker Martin Ritt to Barker's fiction. The film adaptation of *Union Street*, renamed *Stanley and Iris*, may bear little relationship to the original novel, but Barker remembers that Ritt specifically 'identified the exchanges [in the novel] as the kind of thing he remembered from his experience of battle'.[6] Ritt was especially well known as a left-of-centre director whose many political films, from *Edge of the City* (1957) to *The Front* (1976) and finally to *Stanley and Iris*, released in the year of his death, deal with issues of class, racial, and economic exploitation. Ritt had an affinity with the disenfranchised and dispossessed and remains one of the few political filmmakers to work successfully inside Hollywood – just as Barker is one of the few overtly political novelists to find lasting success in the mainstream.

Regeneration was a watershed text, but its popularity reflects a change in direction not for Barker's writing but, more accurately, for the ways in which the popular-cultural history of the war has superseded its social history. Barker published the novel at a point when commemorative and millennial concerns about the First World War were coming to the fore. The novel resonated for readers grappling with a subject disappearing with the last veterans and it immediately became a popular text for school and college students. The reasons for this are clear: the novel is a complex evocation of events that continue to have meaning and there is no narrow nostalgia in Barker's work for the idea of an England that vanished around 1914. This myth of Englishness is so equivocal and inchoate that Barker focuses on it only as it is deemed to touch the lives of her historical characters – W. H. R. Rivers, who at times craves his quiet research in his rooms at Oxford, or Siegfried Sassoon, who remembers his hunting days in rural Kent. In Barker's fictional world, though, Rivers is made to remember that scholarly research involved painful experiments on nerve regeneration. Eschewing nostalgia, Barker has succeeded in playing out the drama of war via demoralized men caught in the exigencies of battle in ways that resonate with contemporary anxieties. She puts Edward Carpenter's idea of the 'love of comrades' to a late-twentieth-century test, in the same way that her study of Craiglockhart Hospital provides a meditative exegesis of poems like Owen's 'Mental Cases'. She also

4

reminds generations for whom the First World War is a distant event that the British cultural landscape was cleaved open by the war. Conflictual class relations resulted in the rise of the Labour Party and only after political upheaval was there a restoration of class differentials, so that by the 1980s, when Barker began to publish, attention to class had once again become unfashionable. John Major spoke of creating a merito-cratic 'classless' society, following his predecessor Margaret Thatcher in proselytizing that the working classes were in a terminable decline along with the industries they had laboured to maintain. Tony Blair's talk of 'ordinary people' living together as 'one nation' fails to acknowledge that a 'median' income and a 'moderate', middle-class lifestyle provide a very partial view of contemporary Britain. In an uncharacteristically clear reference to class, at the 1999 Labour Party Conference Blair declared the 'class war' finally over. Britain has suppos-edly lost its old class consciousness and the term has become synonymous with 'old-style' socialism, another axiom Barker slices her way through with humour and intelligence. How-ever, British society remains hierarchical and stratified and Barker creates characters for whom atavistic class markers continue to matter at specific points in the twentieth century.[7]

Barker does retain a substantial connection with her work-ing-class roots. Consequently, underlying assumptions about the early work set in the north-east were rumblings of Raymond Williams and his designation of mid-nineteenth-century novels as 'industrial novels' and of Arnold Kettle, who famously coined the term 'social-problem novels' to discuss those fictions that deal symptomatically with class in economic and political terms. Working-class writing has traditionally been read as diagnostic.[8] However, when Barker published *Union Street* in 1982 she did not recreate a 'knowable commu-nity' in Williams's sense but a community in transition, located between an industrial past and a post-industrial future. Nor is *Union Street* entirely naturalistic in its narrative strategies either. Barker has never been an uncomplicatedly realist writer, despite the temptation for early reviewers to term her novels 'gritty social realism' without delving beneath the surface expectations of such epithets. The connections between the women in *Union Street* are orchestrated in such a way as to

5

allow characters to merge existentially as well as experientially. Alice Bell, the oldest of the seven women, is privy to the feelings and thoughts of the younger women with whom she shares her environment, not because she knows them but because she has an existential as well as a historicized understanding of each of the changing phases of women's lives in the north-east of England that Barker describes.

The local and regional focus is one aspect of Barker's fiction, but the politics of the novel locate her work in a wider context too, with stark reminders of specific features of national and public memory. Barker's fiction incorporates wide-angled representations and close-up shots of particular historical moments or events, delving into the unresolved tension between memory and history. The case of the Yorkshire Ripper in *Blow Your House Down*, for example, is the model in a narrative that subverts the mystery of male domination and the mystique of male violence. What Barker calls 'the shadow of monstrosities' is cast across more recent novels like *Another World* and *Border Crossing*. Behind the descriptions of anxious parents and violent children is the recognition that the murders committed by Mary Bell, Jon Venables and Robert Thompson, and Fred and Rosemary West have forced the public to rethink its response to contemporary conditions. Violence cannot always be defeated; it exists not only in war or organized crime but in the family, at the heart of society not only at its fraying edges. *Border Crossing* opens with a middle-class marriage in crisis, a suicide attempt in the derelict docklands that border the couple's home, and goes on to map a young murderer's faltering steps towards social rehabilitation. Of course, in the Trilogy, the First World War resonates down the twentieth century, while in *Liza's England* and *The Man Who Wasn't There* the impact of the Second World War dominates. Eric Hobsbawm has famously conflated the two world wars into a single process of warfare, 'a rising curve of barbarism', so that the intervening years are not a hiatus but part of a crisis-ridden 'Age of Catastrophe'.[9] His idea of the 'short' twentieth century is useful when apprehending Barker's keen sense of the rising curve of violence that breaks open the 'the myth – the moral heartland' (*BC* 116), as the character Martha Pitt describes our self-absorbed faith in society in *Border Crossing*. Barker explores the extent to which violence, often casual and sometimes socially sanctioned, impacts on individuals, and how evil can crack open complacency and implicate even the most cautious among us. Violence is endemic in society and so cuts through class and gender barriers.

For Fredric Jameson, history is inaccessible except in textual form, via successive rewritings and overwritings, or interpretations and allegories. Theorist Michel Foucault explains that, in order to create 'grand narratives' of the past as coherent and continuous, one has to ignore the discontinuities and the ruptures in what happened in order to construct a unified view.[10] Barker is not restricted by a teleological line of enquiry; her creative impetus is to narrate through and around history, or to stay in the margins of what has come to be understood as history. If we believe that the historian writes through the lens of his own categories, so too does the novelist – novels often have agendas and preoccupations. For Barker, one such preoccupation, for example, is how gender and class have shaped our understanding of labour and capitalism, warfare and the home front, the family, sex, and reproduction. However, to cling too forcefully to a single item in a writer's lexicon is to miss so much more. For example, when Barker said 'memory is my subject', Suzie MacKenzie seized on the statement to argue that there is nothing predictive in novels that cast back to the past. A closer reading reveals that in Barker's first novel, *Union Street*, Kelly Brown sees her future in the old woman Alice, whom she meets on the last night of the old lady's life, and, in *The Man Who Wasn't There*, Colin Harper meets his own future self. Barker has called the latter her 'what-if book' and it is both experimental and speculative. Similarly, Liza, the octogenarian protagonist of *Liza's England*, retains the kind of faith in the future that her 29-year-old social worker can only marvel at. One critic goes so far as to argue that Liza 'enables Stephen to move forward into his own future'.[11] Barker is a supremely contemporary novelist for whom the present – and the future – are founded on the past. Like Nobel-prize winner William Faulkner, for whom the Old Slave South infiltrated his apprehension of a new and evolving American South, in Barker's fiction 'the past isn't over, it isn't even past'. Or, as Albert Einstein aphoristically put it, 'the distinction between past, present and future is only an illusion, even if a stubborn one'.[12] In *Border Crossing*, the young man in his twenties who murdered an elderly lady when he was just 12 years old lives every day with the memory of that event. The act of murder dogs his future. Of his victim he says: 'I don't fight her now. She's got a right to quite a few of my brain cells' (*BC* 215).

Barker refuses to flatten out complexities. Not only do we cling to patterns in life, but in our reading we cling to metaphors, seeking out the 'rules' of experience that confirm readerly expectations. When these seem too neat or obligatory, Barker may sidestep our expectation, deflect our anticipation, or undermine the very metaphor on which we have begun to base our interpretation of a novel. For example, the idea of inserting one's hand into a bayonet wound – something that Barker herself did as a child to experience her grandfather's war wound sensorially – is first mentioned in *Liza's England*, when Liza goes to work for a butcher who suffered such a wound. Later it is placed under scrutiny in *The Man Who Wasn't There*. Colin, a 'Doubting Thomas' – who 'believed nothing till he'd *poked* his fingers into the Lord's wounds', is made to understand that one does not have to see to believe (*MWWT* 111). Even if the physical wound is determined, its meaning may not be. Later still, in *Another World*, Barker returns to the same metaphor when Geordie Lucas feels he is dying from a bayonet wound more than seventy years after it was inflicted. What he feels does not change the fact that cancer is overtaking his body, but Geordie's self-diagnosis is no less true; what finally dispatches the old soldier is his belief that the psychological repercussions of the war are written on the body. It is part of the practice of a writer to recall and rework scenes, creating a sense of textuality across novels, but in Barker the process also serves as a reminder that whatever happens will reveal itself more fully with time.

The meanings novels produce are inherently plural and contradictory, as are their characters. Billy Prior, a curious mixture of fastidiousness and aggression, is the nearest we have to a main protagonist across the Trilogy. Introduced as one of Rivers's patients in *Regeneration*, his conflicting beliefs and experiences become the driving force of *The Eye in the Door* and his return to the Western Front dominates *The Ghost Road*. For this reader he is also the most Barkeresque of characters in that he can be read as a composite. His inception can be located as evolving out of Colin in *The Man Who Wasn't There*, through Stephen in *Liza's England*, and in another incarnation he evolves into Geordie in *Another World*. Danny Miller's confrontation with his psychologist in *Border Crossing* is strongly reminiscent of the borders crossed by Prior in his sessions with Rivers, though Prior is never so chilling. Historical figures like Rivers and Sassoon may seem to stand outside this tendency, but they too are endowed with as much imaginative force as the fictive Billy Prior. Barker has described the novel as 'the only art form that allows you to think analytically while feeling deeply simultaneously',[13] and she keys into contemporary debates. In the Trilogy it is the psychological chaos of war that interests Barker most of all, through victims of 'shell shock' or neurasthenia and attendant conditions relating to the repression of memory and soldiers' experiences 'out there', issues that came back into public consciousness with the Gulf War. Psychology is a science of the imagination and it is through dialogue, Barker's abiding strength, that she probes psychological realism most fully. She is interested in what fiction can uncover about the kinds of analytical problems that psychologists try to solve. As Dennis Brown argues in 'Self at War', war experience in particular 'has acted as a detonator whereby mental surfaces are broken up, apocalypse is discovered . . . and disintegration is plumbed beneath layers of self-ordering'.[14] From W. H. R. Rivers in the Trilogy to Tom Seymour the child psychologist in *Border Crossing*, Barker charts some of the changes in popular psychiatry over the twentieth century.

In fact, Barker began exploring the psychological effects of rape on the child Kelly in *Union Street* and the emotional impact on Jean of having killed an innocent man in *Blow Your House Down*. As Nicole Ward Jouve has argued, fiction is probably the only medium through which working-class characters and prostitutes like Jean and Brenda are lifted out of objectification and speechlessness and given back the humanity that society more generally denies them.[15] What people often choose not to see, the taboos that discomfort and

2

Stories of 'the other Britain': *Union Street* and *Blow Your House Down*

Articulation is the tongue-tied's fighting.
(Tony Harrison, 'On Not Being Milton', 1978)

STORIES FROM THE MARGINS

Theologist Michael I. Bochenski commends Barker's early work for bringing home to a wide spectrum of readers that poverty and deprivation still obtain in contemporary Britain. He describes her novels as 'stories of the other Britain, the one that many never see or never want to realize exists'.[1] This raises a significant if problematic point: however laudatory, the praise risks marginalizing the fiction, setting it outside mainstream experience and appeal. It also invests Barker's fiction with a sociological imperative, the very same label that defines as 'political' narratives that tell stories of the underclass but normalizes as 'universal' stories of middle- or upper-class protagonists. For Bochenski, however, the real emphasis lies with how important it remains to tell stories against the grain, to unsettle complacency. One is reminded of Elaine Showalter's prediction in 1977 that in the work of contemporary women writers 'feminine realism, feminist protest and female self-analysis are combining in the context of twentieth-century social and political concern' in order to shatter such complacency:

11

There is a female voice that has rarely spoken for itself in the English novel – the voice of the shopgirl and the charwoman, the housewife and the barmaid. One possible effect of the women's movement might be the broadening of the class base from which women novelists [and their characters] have come.[2]

Pat Barker fulfils many of Showalter's hopes. The Fawcett Society Book Prize for *Union Street* singled it out as the best book to make a 'substantial contribution to the understanding of women's position in society today'.[3] Barker also inevitably tussles with what is salient in Bochenski's and Showalter's assertions – political and feminist claims for knowledge.

In *Union Street* Barker shows how the politicization of working-class experience failed to advance the lot of working-class women. Nell Dunn's novel *Up the Junction*, filmed as long ago as 1965 by Ken Loach, and to critical acclaim, explored the lives of women factory workers in Battersea. Tellingly, *Up the Junction* includes the kind of back-street abortion that Barker reworks in *Union Street*, a novel she set in the early 1970s and published a decade later. Of Wharfe Street, where some of her characters live before moving into Union Street, she says, 'suicide, mental illness, crime, incest had flourished there' (*US* 74). It is the site of the abortion: Iris King, who believes she has successfully escaped Wharfe Street, finds herself back there in a desperate bid to save her youngest daughter from becoming a child-mother. The fact that abortion became legal in Britain in 1967 is shown to have little or no impact on Barker's women characters. The energy of the 1960s – the visibility of the working class, feminist activism, and the politicized reaction of mass audiences to harrowing tales like *Cathy Come Home* (1966) and *Up the Junction* – has failed to transform the lives of women in *Union Street* or *Blow Your House Down*. Joanne Wilson, living on Union Street in the 1970s and pregnant, tells her student boyfriend: 'And if you're thinking of hot baths and gin, well, for a kickoff it doesn't work. If it did I wouldn't be here for one. And in the second place, we haven't got a bath, you daft bugger. If I start boiling meself to death in front of the fire don't you think me Mam'ld notice?' (*US* 98). Focusing on the north-east, Barker excavates the lives of women whose roles often divide them from men, and in *Blow Your House Down* she presents an excoriating exposé of sex work, revealing how incredibly close the prostitutes' experience is to the mindless and physically numbing work performed by women in a chicken factory.

WOMEN TALKING

In a 1987 edition of the BBC programme *Bookmark* Barker restated that working-class women are articulate, creative, and an appropriate subject for serious fiction. But no one had been listening to their voices. Barker sees her work as originating in an oral tradition of articulate working-class tellers of stories. She provides an unqualified and unapologetic focus on the voices of those who have received scant recognition or celebration in the English literary tradition, just as Showalter predicted. Raymond Williams reminds us in his essay 'Structures of Feeling' of those social groups whose language may not allow for the complete articulation of their experiences. When the discourse available to them fails, their voices exist 'at the very edge of semantic availability'. Williams calls attention to the making of one's identity *through* language.[4] Social groups can become 'aphasic' when denied access to the orthodox language structures that define their reality. Barker's women are subalterns (a term first coined by Antonio Gramsci to describe those groups stifled by a capitalist ruling class) who tenaciously break out of the societal patterns that hide their reality. For example, the social security visitors to elderly Alice Bell, with 'the posh voices, the questions, the eyes everywhere', are dehumanized, reduced to synecdoche, while Alice's response, 'them buggers have been here again', is a strengthening of her determination to continue to exist outside any official assessment of her needs (*US* 233).

Barker's women speak in realistic dialogue that has consistently been praised by readers and critics alike. D. J. Taylor cites Barker as a writer concerned to 'establish a prose that reflects "ordinary" speech' and Anne Boston of *New Society* credited her with giving 'an authentic voice to the lives of the poor and dispossessed as few other English contemporary novelists have managed to do'.[5] Class and experience are embedded in language and one has only to listen to the prostitutes in

Barker's second novel to hear characters speaking with a subjectivity that confounds generalized bigotry. Jean addresses the reader directly: 'You do a lot of walking in this job. More than you might think. In fact, when I get to the end of a busy Saturday night, it's me feet that ache. There, that surprised you, didn't it? (BYHD 94). In one of the most illuminating readings of Barker's early fiction, Peter Hitchcock argues that it is the communality of the language and the experiences that this may convey that give the narrative its 'politico-aesthetic strength'.[6]

Barker reinforces the articulacy of those who have been traditionally rendered silent and deemed inarticulate, but it would be too simple to say her characters speak themselves into being. Barker is fascinated by the *problems* of communication. Communicative failure that she explores most famously in the Trilogy via stammering and mute soldiers can be traced back to her earliest work. In *Union Street*, John Scaife finds his speech blocked when a blood clot forms in his chest, and Alice Bell, suffering the effects of a stroke, battles against expressive aphasia. Eleven-year-old Kelly Brown remains silent, telling nobody she has been raped until three weeks after the ordeal. Then she acts out her pain by breaking into family homes and defacing her classroom while locked into silence. Although her neighbours sympathize, the little girl 'has moved beyond the range of its [the street's] understanding' (US 51). The reading may seem bleak, but Barker shows that easy community – the working classes in and out of each others' houses to borrow a cup of sugar or for emotional sustenance – is a fallacy.

In Barker's novels women are not celebrated in a feminist reclamation of sisterhood or class solidarity; women can be sour and dour. They often fail even to allow for similarities in their experiences. Like Iris Marion Young in a well-known essay, Barker elucidates the ways in which sisterhood forms part of 'an unrealistic vision for transformative politics in mass urban society'. Despite Simone de Beauvoir's idea of women creating a 'counter-universe' and Nina Auerbach's idea of an 'anti-society', Barker's women are rarely seen to form genuine friendships or maintain supportive mother–daughter bonds into adulthood.[7] When her husband dies, Muriel Scaife finds her mother minimizes her loss, and Barker's irony is barbed: 'The old lady's conviction that her son-in-law had enjoyed excellent health, though a little shaken by his death, was by no means overcome' (*US* 170). In *Blow Your House Down*, Brenda's mother-in-law, Edith, worships her indolent son and is dismissive of the daughters who care and clean for her. The reader is prevented from falling into any easy moral rectitude that might assume that women suffering similar deprivations will come together in vocal support of one another. This is not usually the case. They often speak disparagingly of each other ('sometimes I wonder why I lower myself to speak to her' (*US* 78)) and judge each other quite harshly. For example, most deem Kelly's mother a 'bad' mother, and, although she crosses the street to Iris King's home in search of moral support following Kelly's rape, Mrs Brown wonders 'what on earth had possessed her to come ... the version that went the rounds wouldn't be fair on her' (*US* 41). Barker gives the lie to comfortable myths of working-class warmth and harmony.

In fact, Barker's early fiction disturbs any comfortable slippage into a middle-class perspective on working-class lives. Barker admits the middle-class person is 'an absent character with whom you are actively discouraged from identifying. The schoolteacher or social worker may make an appearance but I conceived of *Union Street* as a vat with smooth curving sides. Once you are in the vat, you are in working-class life, and there is no relief' (AI). For example, the openings of both *Union Street* and *Blow Your House Down* involve similar descriptions of bedrooms that young sisters share. In *Union Street* a square of cardboard covers over a broken window but barely saves Kelly or her sister from the cold. In *Blow Your House Down*, to manoeuvre one's way into the room between two single beds and a wardrobe, one has to stand sideways and shuffle. In the smallest of ways the texture of Barker's prose bespeaks the circumscribed lives of an underclass. Lives are lived in such close proximity that the most intimate of functions, like time spent in the bathroom or menstruation, become topics for heated family argument. The reader is caught inside a closed private world, as inside the vat of Barker's metaphor.

Barker is a writer whose fiction began to make its mark in Left and feminist circles in the 1980s in Britain, a period of narrow and reductive social policies on the Right and local community ideals on the Left. It was a period in which feminists began to test theories about women's lives against material conditions and to celebrate those writers whose fiction articulated specifically female experiences. This rendered her a significant novelist for the Virago imprint and she stayed with the feminist publishing house for her first three novels. One is reminded reading these novels of those characters George Orwell failed to give much time to in *The Road to Wigan Pier* (1937) – working-class women. Mrs Brooker, his landlady, is an invalid, but Orwell never troubles to discover her condition. Rather, he puts it down to over-eating and her 'self-pitying talk' revolts him. Emmie cleans his room but is simply a 'sharp-nosed, unhappy-looking girl who worked at one of the mills for some starvation wage'. In fact, a 'slum girl' who catches his eye from a train window gains more of his attention and receives more sympathy.[8] It would have been something of an epiphany for Orwell to notice and to choose to include the kinds of details that Barker opens up with regard to Kelly Brown. Barker's concern with the gender blindness of acclaimed writers like Orwell involves her in a kind of recovery of those silenced in much previous writing. It is the kind of retrieval that has proved very important for women writers and readers, though some have labelled it nostalgic.[9] But, like D. H. Lawrence, whom she believes 'casts a long shadow', Barker has the creative energy to break open certain established literary tropes and reconfigure the contexts in which working-class lives may be understood. In her early work, Barker takes as a major theme the disintegration of northern industrial communities in the 1970s and its repercussions in relationships between women *and* men. It is this which particularizes the force and power of novels in which local communities battle for survival, and which draws out the relationship between visibility and vulnerability in her portrayal of the men in *Union Street*.

DISPOSSESSED MEN IN A POST-INDUSTRIAL WASTELAND

Union Street, described as a 'long overdue working-class masterpiece' by the *New Statesman*, was published in the year of the Anglo-Argentine war over the Falklands, in the decade of Thatcher and Reagan and media soundbites on a 'classless society'. It examines 1973 through the lens of the 1980s and locates the year within a broad socio-cultural understanding of the era. In the 'winter of discontent' of 1971–2 unemployment had risen to its highest since the Second World War. The Heath Government found itself in dispute with the TUC and strikes followed, so that many Britons spent the winter with only sporadic electricity and water supplies. The novel's political and geographical location is specific though by no means overburdened by topical references. There are unaffected nods to issues that dominated the news at the time – striking miners, the Troubles in Northern Ireland, huge increases in the price of petrol.[10] The narrative explores what a 'post-industrial' world may mean for individuals and communities who have traditionally relied on the manufacturing industries for their social presence and regional pride, as well as for their material and economic survival.

The novel is set in a 'steel town' and, when the steelworks closes, the men who have stoked the furnace for more than a century are displaced; they haunt the labour exchanges, but their labour power ceases to have any exchange value. The tragedy of dispossession is male: hard-working John Scaife, laid off and dying of a work-related medical condition, is paralysed when he finds himself unable to find common ground with his son by explaining 'the world of work'. Young men like Lisa Goddard's husband Brian are suffering long-term unemployment following redundancy and their wives bear the brunt of their despair. Lisa feels his powerlessness and sees his personal dissolution: 'At the finish he was walking round and round the sofa like somebody caged' (*US* 120). Men, denuded by the collapse of heavy industries in the north, are disempowered patriarchs, but they are not uniformly de-monized. Brian Goddard is violent when drunk and his wife Lisa suffers for his unwillingness to communicate, but John and Muriel Scaife enjoy a loving, supportive relationship until his premature death. The men's location on the vulnerable edge of the family unit had not been represented in British popular culture, except, perhaps, for those of David Storey's characters poised for flight, until Alan Bleasdale's *Boys From the Blackstuff*, which hit television screens in the same year

Union Street was published. Novels by James Kelman tackle similar subject matter and films like *Brassed Off* (1996), tackling pit closures, and *The Full Monty* (1997), in which redundant Sheffield steelworkers become strippers, use comedy to intervene in real social problems.

Barker is iconoclastic: she sought to address the issues facing disenfranchised men from her first published novel and yet she has been accused of privileging women over men in her early work. Critics from Jeremy Seabrook to Ian Haywood misread *Union Street*, believing that 'male characters and masculinity are . . . "written off" '.[11] How should the reader get to grips with such contradictions? To follow Haywood's line is tacitly to presuppose that 'working class' retains connotations of masculinity and silently elides women. But, more importantly, it is to fail to note that it is precisely the absence of paid labour for the men in Barker's novels that shifts them to the margins of working-class consciousness. Masculinity – like class as a descriptor – is neither unitary nor fixed and the meanings attached to male experiences have altered significantly over the course of the twentieth century. Barker makes it clear that the collapse of heavy industry foreshadows the collapse of socially integrated male identities. The men folk are pushed to the *symbolic* edges of the text, where they hover like spectres on a barren industrial wasteland: they have not been airbrushed out of the text. On the contrary, they have been relegated to the fringes of society by a series of governmental and technological changes, the after effects of which are represented here. The effect of the men's displacement on the women is marked, and from the Goddards to the Harrisons the rift between men and women is shown to be widening.

George Harrison is conveyed via a sustained evocation of his interior life. He has retired after forty years working at the blast furnaces. His wife cannot bear him to be under her feet all day. She cleans around him, so, like the younger unemployed men, he spends little time at home, sitting in the park or in the library, until he takes a job cleaning public toilets. When he meets Blonde Dinah, 'a legend' after forty years as a prostitute, he comes to the realization that for Dinah sex might be a job, like cleaning lavatories. Having drawn our attention to George's lonely life and faded marriage, during which he has never seen his wife naked, Barker ensures that he discovers sex with Dinah, and more. There is pathos, pride, shame, and amusement in this short section of the novel, the very emotions George knows he will feel when looking back on their encounter. The coming-together of an elderly man and woman on a dark night energizes the man and restores to him a sense of life-renewing potency. Dinah is conveyed sympathetically through George's narration but Dinah also foreshadows those prostitutes like Kath in *Blow Your House Down* who also fail to find lasting companionship. As always, Dinah wakes alone.

The sequence in which George and Dinah fleetingly come together exemplifies a largely unspoken need for social and sexual contact, but Barker refuses to elevate any one character's needs over those of any other. Importantly, there is no single female protagonist for the reader to identify as representative in *Union Street*; promoting empathy with a single idiosyncratic character might also serve to alienate her from those around her. Instead, Barker charts a working-class continuum, through the lives and memories of seven women, ascending in age, who inhabit the same terraced street and whose lives draw on a century's experience of girlhood and womanhood, which incorporates their relationships with men. She traces these women finally to old age and death. Alice Bell, the oldest of the street's inhabitants, has battled to stay out of the workhouse and continues to fight to retain her independence, outside the nursing home for the elderly that occupies the spot where the workhouse once stood. Alice relives the past in her worries about the instabilities of contemporary Britain and her diminished importance within it. Finally she chooses suicide, rather than death from hypothermia in the old house she scrimped to buy but can no longer afford to heat. Suicide is the nearest she can muster to taking control of her own future. Barker pulls no punches – neither with Alice nor with Kelly, who, once raped, is bitter in a way that connects intimately with Alice's final resolution of her pain and anguish. They meet in the park where Alice intends to sit in the cold – to meet it rather than succumb to it – until the cold penetrates to her very bones and kills her:

'I used to come her when I was a little lass, aye, younger than you.' The old woman looked with dim eyes around the park. Kelly followed her gaze and, for the first time in her life, found it possible to believe than an old woman had once been a child. At the same moment, and also for the first time, she found it possible to believe in her own death. There was terror in this, but no sadness. She stared at the old woman, as if she held, and might communicate, the secret of life. (*US* 67)

Barker is attempting a distillation of historical and class memory, of the national with the personal. This is an idea she develops later in the more lyrical *Liza's England* (formerly known as *The Century's Daughter*[12]). Liza Jarrett Wright, born on the eve of the twentieth century, grapples with the vicissitudes of the 1980s while picking her way back through her memories of earlier decades, before dying at the hands of a gang of dispossessed young men who break into her home. Liza is an extension of Alice, and the unrelenting inequities she suffers a decade later are testament to the disintegrating sense of personal safety and social security that coloured the last decades of the twentieth century. It is a topic to which Barker returns in *Another World* and *Border Crossing*.

WOMEN AND SEX WORK

In the first instance, the drama of violent encounters is most trenchantly played out in *Blow Your House Down*. A group of prostitutes stalked by a serial killer are herded into one area of town, 'Northgate'. The police increase arrests for soliciting in other areas in order to pen the women – or 'bait', as one character terms them – into a single zone the police can watch, waiting for the next attack. This strategy echoes one of the ways that police took to regulating prostitution in Bradford when the man who was later discovered to be Peter Sutcliffe succeeded in holding a community in a stranglehold of fear. When 'The Yorkshire Ripper', Peter Sutcliffe, stalked Leeds and the north-west from 1975 to 1981, he left thirteen women dead and at least seven more badly injured. One of Barker's minor characters 'lived' through Bradford and has tales to tell of clients pretending to be 'the Ripper' to scare the women just for fun (*BYHD* 12–13). As one reads into Barker's novel, one is instantly reminded of the media representation of Jack the

Ripper's Whitechapel murders in the 1880s and the way in which the same macabre press invested the murderer with a powerful mystique on which the public could draw. 'Jack the Ripper' was media-made and he continues to live in the popular imagination providing the model for – often sensationalist – representations of the psychopathic killer to this day. The media representations of Peter 'the Ripper' Sutcliffe and the women he murdered incensed Barker, who realized that attributing serial killers with a pet name distances them from their reality as males. She purposely undercuts tabloid depictions of serial killers as asocial monsters, so that the unnamed man who stalks the women in *Blow Your House Down* retains his specificity as a man, as 'Somebody's Husband, Somebody's Son', to borrow the title of Gordon Burns's 1984 study of Sutcliffe.

Office cleaner Olive Smelt, scarred by Sutcliffe, was found by a 'woman acquaintance' on Friday, 15 August 1975. Police suspected her husband of the crime. She, rather than Sutcliffe, becomes a much more important model for Barker in her portrayal of battered Maggie as discovered by prostitute Brenda. Barker takes the bare facts and opens them out to scrutiny.[13] She places her women victims and their friends at the centre of the text and reaffirms their humanity in the face of abuse – and in the face of the Ripper myth. The myth that emerged in the twentieth century was based on a battle between a predatory man and 'fallen' women; after slashing his victims' throats, the original Ripper surgically removed the women's uteruses. The nineteenth-century media managed their coverage as melodrama, warning 'good' women that 'bad' women were powerless to protect themselves from a punishment with which they colluded if they lived outside the safety of marriage and family.[14]

Clive Bloom, discussing Jack the Ripper, has argued that the psychopath and the prostitute were 'two ends of a society that refused to acknowledge their presence'. Invisible and located 'on the edge of the rational' in his reading,[15] the danger is that both will seem removed from societal norms. On the contrary, it is to their sheer ordinariness that Barker pays attention in *Blow Your House Down*, refusing to transcend their specificities in symbolic interplay.[16] Barker's Ripper suffers from halitosis and sucks Parma violets, a sweet-smelling lozenge, to mask his bad breath. The reader discovers he has had a religious upbringing and his smarting hatred of women is touched off easily, by a woman's song or her laugh. Most importantly, the novel is not 'about' the killer: it may ostensibly work as a thriller but clues lead the reader on a false trail. Nor is it about the detectives bent on tracking the serial killer down. The story is told from the women's points of view. Despite the title's reference to the fairy story of the 'Three Little Pigs' and the wolf that huffed and puffed to blow down the home designed to afford them lasting safety, the story remains with his victims. One comes to realize that the women will endure, through Brenda, and through Jean and Maggie. Maggie is left reconfirming her trust in and love for husband Bill, and Jean carries the dilemma of the text. If the novel is an urban fairy tale, it is so in so far as this spirited morality tale takes place in a squalid urban environment. The familiarity of the dank viaduct, derelict factory yards, and boarded-up streets extends the northern landscape beyond the 'Lowryscape' that Philip Dodd describes as 'a settled place with an agreed iconography'.[17] Barker delivers a searing picture of the physical environment in which the women work.

There are a number of reasons why Barker has been claimed as a feminist writer, and, in her early work, the emphasis on sexual politics is a clear feminist marker. Barker critiques those social institutions that confine young lives and elicit false expectations – marriage and work as well as the ideology of family as the building block of civilized society. Brenda and Brian feel that marriage ended their lives, his at 19, hers at 16, but motherhood continues to be Brenda's strongest emotional tie and motivator. She feels she has lost a part of herself the first time she leaves the children to go to the factory. She manages until she is sacked and has a hard time beginning a life of sex work. She is violated on her first nervous outing with a client who has 'a field day': 'He'd have done it in her lugs if they had been the right shape. She fell out of the car two hours later, too shocked to cry . . .'. Brenda is swept up by Kath, who forces her to learn a hard lesson: 'Look love, you want to run your cunt like a soup kitchen . . . you don't do it from here' (*BYHD* 45). Brenda suffers a series of wrenches that pull her away from adolescent ideas of what a young woman should expect her life to be. But she adapts. Barker intercuts Brenda's formative experiences – of marriage, motherhood, factory work, and prostitution – with her seasoned observations on life and society. Barker refuses to fix Brenda into paradigmatic formulations of mother or whore; to do so would be to render her allegorical or representative. There are no 'fallen women' or 'pretty women' with hearts of gold in this novel and prostitutes are neither symbolic of sin nor subjects for romance. The women who meet in the Palmerston public house form a heterogeneous group. If Brenda expresses the decision to work as economic, Jean articulates a very different ideology ('I like this life. I'm not in it because I'm a poor, deprived, inadequate, half-witted woman, whatever some people might like to think, I'm in it because it suits me . . . I like the freedom' (*BYHD* 112)). Carol is attracted to the money but shuns the lifestyle and only Dave and Elaine fall into the expected formulation of pimp and prostitute.

The women characters extend literary examinations of working-class women. In this late-twentieth-century context, if Barker's women signify anything other than themselves, it is through the political statements the novel makes in its reaction *against* theorizing labour and sexuality in ways that undervalue working-class lives and *against* the silent prejudice that surrounds women in sex work. None of the women professes any sexual pleasure and the scenes in which sex is performed are cold and bleak: 'She braced herself against the wall. It'd have to be a knee-wobbler: she was damned if she was gunna lie down in all that muck' (*BYHD* 43). Barker's critique of patriarchal devices is direct: in the chicken factory, 'killing's for the men', whilst the women tend to the poultry, cleaning and trussing the birds. They soon learn to 'whistle through' their work, turning chickens out at the end of production tidily trussed once they have 'the knack'. The women's capacity to adapt is as clear in the factory as on the streets. The women stand in the shadow of the chicken factory and Barker's exegesis of the relationship between the modes of production and her characters' thin, meagre lives is exemplified through Brenda, who, after a broken marriage, turns to the production lines in the factory to support herself and her children but finds Northgate 'more honest' in the end. After tussles with the factory management and with the social services, she chooses the sex industry over factory work:

> What got her was the hypocrisy of it all. They went on about being married, but when you got right down to it ... what they [the social services] really thought was: if you're getting on your back for a fella, he ought to pay ... You might just as well be standing on a street corner in bloody Northgate – at least it'd be honest. (*BYHD* 30)

Similarly, where race and racism complicate Barker's traditionally white working-class framework, she provides some short but telling descriptions. For Brenda in *Blow Your House Down*, the Pakistani women who live on her street are invisible – largely because orphan Brenda has no experience of the resilience of a community structure on which to draw. Instead, she falls into dismissive stereotyping: 'you saw the men come and go, but not the women' (*US* 21). Similarly, she fails to lodge her children with an African Caribbean childminder, choosing instead a white woman who abuses them. Barker is not a writer who opens out discussions of race relations in new ways. Rather she represents in direct terms the kinds of incidents that give the lie to this society's multiculturalism.

VIOLENT ENCOUNTERS

What is most marked in *Blow Your House Down*, though, is the unblinking way that Barker tackles the barbaric violence that her subject matter demands. Fettered by social expectation and mired in poverty, characters also learn that violence is a very real facet of daily life. Barker pulls no punches. When choosing to depict violence against women, there are a number of problems that any writer faces. Graphic descriptions of brutality may alienate the reader, especially when the perpetrator's point of view is also conveyed and the reader risks identifying with his anger or lust for power. Identifying with the victim is equally unsettling when the reader is powerless to intervene but is positioned as witness or voyeur: the horror of the scene may fascinate as well as appal. A further issue that complicates descriptions of misogynistic violence is the author who explains or accounts for violence in sociological terms in order to justify its place in the text. Barker negotiates the pitfalls and succeeds in involving the reader without alienating her *in Blow Your House Down*. The single most violent scene is Kath's gruesome death at the hands of her dispatcher, a killer for whom 'it feels right'. But at the scene's heart is the simple line 'At some point, unnoticed by him, Kath died' (*BYHD* 64). In this sequence the omniscient narrator is unobtrusive and there is no pre-emptive strike on the emotions. What is undermined is the reader's ability to skim over what happens to Kath. As Barker has admitted, 'If you hate violence, it is always easiest to try to grasp for a solution' (AI). Here none is forthcoming: there is no rational explanation for the horror. The most the reader can begin to rationalize is that hearing Kath drunkenly singing a hymn sparks off a distorted memory in her assailant. But, finally, Kath is a prostitute and the unnamed man a killer of prostitutes. No more than this underpins the evil at the heart of his actions. In the meantime, the reader has already become implicated in the crime. Barker shifts in and out of Kath's perspective ('Oh God. She landed herself a real nutter this time. *Give him what he wants'*) to the killer's ('In his mind's eye he could see his buttocks labouring in and out. Ridiculous. It was no good. He fell forward . . .'). In passages like the one in which Kath dies, Barker lays bare subjects that are almost too distressing to contemplate. The voyeurism inherent in the act of reading fixes the reader firmly in the scene: there is little extraneous description and the environment shrinks to the space in which the murder takes place, the old mattress and what it holds: 'If you approached the mattress casually you would see nothing but a heap of old rags. You would tread on her before you realized a woman's body lay there' (*BYHD* 65). The use of the second person 'you' and the present continuous heightens the reader's closeness to what has occurred.

HUMOUR IN ADVERSITY

Barker's work can be achingly funny even when the topics she explores are frightening and violent. She is particularly sharp in her deconstruction of gender roles. Stark humour that carries the shock of recognition exists alongside the dry and understated. In *Union Street* Mrs Harrison's campaign against dirt and wantonness is a case in point. She walks the streets collecting used condoms because they ignite the mission fire so quickly. She uses sugar tongs to pick them up because only her husband uses sugar. Iris King's bitter 'I took a meat cleaver to him', alluding to her husband's attempts to offer her to his drunken friends for sex, exemplifies the line that Barker is able to walk between humour and sexual violence. She is a rare writer. In *Blow Your House Down*, Brenda's mother-in-law's grotesque character is firmly based in a carefully observed critique of gender relations. Edith regularly dusts her husband in the same way that she cleans her home; she will not let him leave the home unchecked. With hindsight, Brenda is convinced that his daily trips to the pub are a cover for the comfort of sex with prostitutes: 'You couldn't blame him, mind. If he'd got it out at home, she'd have only dusted it' (*BYHD* 21). Barker's wry reading of the interrelationship of family and fornication, patriarchy and parsimony, fuels her interrogation of social ritual. Ada Lumb in *The Ghost Road* is a variation on Edith. A grotesque figure, she reads the penny dreadfuls, flirts with Billy Prior, yet thwarts every attempt he and her daughter Sarah have for a moment alone, even though they have become engaged to be married and have precious little time together before he returns to the Front. Barker explores working-class lives with searing humour, especially through the minor characters that she limns out with a few deft strokes. Brenda's parents-in-law are minor characters, referenced only in the exposition of Brenda's paltry experience of family life, but, in context, Barker captures a marriage that endures in the midst of family factions, foibles, and secrets. Brenda pronounces the family 'mad', but behind the candid aplomb is a more acerbic assessment of the ways in which mendacity is pervasive. Even the most swiftly sketched characters harbour secrets and selfish wiles, an idea that Barker extends with her imaginative reading of the contemporary family in *Another World*.

In *Blow Your House Down* Barker points up the differences between what the women characters experience and what they divulge about their experiences. The women are victims of male violence, but they often use humour to defuse the anxiety and anger they feel. Most importantly, as a group the women are not afraid but as individuals they are terrified. As she has stipulated about the prostitutes who gather at Beatie's pub, their communal voice can deny their individual voices (AI).

Cumulatively in the early work, Barker builds a sense of character and context from the inside out. One clear narrative strategy is to move out from the home to wider social relations, but Barker never strays far from the interior lives of her subjects; their anxieties and thwarted aspirations leak into even the most descriptive passages. In *Blow Your House Down*, Jean's histrionic voice pricks the reader: 'you feel yourself getting thinner and thinner, more and more transparent, until every nerve and bone and muscle is laid bare' (*BYHD* 135). Jean has entangled herself in the Nietzschean knot alluded to in the epigraph from *Beyond Good and Evil* (1886): 'Whoever fights monsters should see to it that in the process he does not become a monster. And when you look long into an abyss the abyss also looks into you.' Trying to enter the serial killer's mind, Jean ends up murdering an ordinary 'punter': her need for vengeance has warped her judgement. Through Jean's confiding and confessional first-person narration the reader is implicated in her mistake, catapulted into the realization that anger and fear can beget action. The reader is uncompromisingly trapped in her world. With Barker's third novel, *Liza's England*, the emphasis on character-driven fiction continues and is present to full effect.

3

'You don't kill time, time kills you': Storytelling and *Liza's England*

> A people without a history
> Is not redeemed from time, for history is a patter
> Of timeless moments. So while the light fails
> On a winter's afternoon, in a secluded chapel
> History is now and England.
>
> (T. S. Eliot, 'Little Gidding', 1942)

HISTORY AS CONTINUUM

In *Liza's England* Barker deploys an image of a slag heap as Lloyd George's 'land fit for heroes to live in' (*LE* 159) and later transposes it with an image of the miners' strike and of barbed wire fences enclosing 'work yards that would never work again': 'The wind keened across the brown land, and it seemed to Liza that it lamented vanished communities, scattered families, extinguished fires. Mourned the men who'd crowded on to the ferry boat, at each and every change of shift . . .' (*LE* 216). Images of an industrial wasteland are threaded along the story of Liza Jarret Wright, born on the stroke of midnight in 1900, who tells the story of her life as she has lived it down the twentieth century. The century Liza details is, as Eric Hobsbawm has argued, one of extremes. She loses a brother and a son in the First and Second World Wars, 'a black wind had blown a generation away' (*LE* 275). She suffers poverty and finds her political activism curtailed by penury, and by the

28

1980s, when the novel opens, is living in a condemned terraced street waiting to die.

Liza Wright may be 'the century's daughter' (the original title of Barker's novel) but it is to the final year of her life that Barker turns first. The novel is set in 1984–5 at the height of Thatcherism and amidst the lows of long-term unemployment: a year of strikes and angry demonstrations like the one in which police officer Keith Blakelock was killed. On the one hand, Liza's life is small in scope: she has moved no more than four miles from the place she was born. She has been living in the house she occupies at her death since 1922. In old age she divides her time between the bed and the chair in her cramped living room. On the other hand, her memories open on to a vast world that is epic in scope, 'the long country of the past'. As the octogenarian casts back in time, her box of keepsakes becomes a psychodramatic prop she uses to enter the country of the mind. Lyn Pykett refers to the box as an objective correlative for Liza's matrilineal heritage.[1] Liza explains that it was handed down via her grandmother, but her own mother's cruelty, a recurring motif in the novel, gives the lie to any utopian expression of matrilineage. There are moments in the novel when women come together in union: Liza and Mrs Dobbin are the kind of neighbours for whom a rattle on the fire grate is a call for help that is always answered and Lisa Lowe and Liza support each other in grief after the death of their sons. But, more accurately, the box is a symbol of hidden history. The faded picture on its lid and sides is of women dancing, but it is so 'filmed with dirt' that Liza's gay social worker, Stephen, to whom she shows the box, has difficulty deciding whether some of the figures are men or women (LE 7). The picture would seem to represent both women and men whose lives have been hidden in the trammels of history and Stephen sees himself represented there. Theirs is history as penumbra, lived out in the shadows rather than made by the winners. The memories the box releases are not generally nostalgic either. Liza is much more critical: 'I try to remember what it was really like. Women wore out by the time they were thirty' (LE 218). The past imposes constraints on the present that cannot be brushed away but Liza's memories ease the task she has in hand – her dying – and help her to reflect on the historical contingencies that have shaped her life.

As Liza's life comes to an end, she is invested with what Walter Benjamin in 'The Storyteller' describes as an authority borrowed from death: 'Death is the sanction of everything that the storyteller can tell.'[2] Liza is a chronicler, like Benjamin's 'history-teller', who is less burdened by the need to explain than to *interpret* her life in twentieth-century England. Liza comes to understand herself in and through narrative, or, as Iris Murdoch, novelist and philosopher, puts it in 'Against Dryness', 'through literature we can re-discover a sense of the density of our lives'. Murdoch is advocating the novel form as a means through which to apprehend the complexity of moral life.[3] Liza is one of Barker's most engaging characters: she is venerated, as is Geordie Lucas, the centenarian of *Another World*. She is also distinguished by an elemental life force ('No point being eighty is there . . . if you can't be a bit outrageous' (*LE* 1)). Liza is sharp and dryly acerbic. Of the doctor who assessed her capabilities she says, 'He asked such bloody stupid questions: who was the Prime Minister. I told him I was trying to forget' (*LE* 19).

In literature the aged have traditionally been occluded as complex, sexual, intellectual beings: few writers have devoted much serious time to the elderly as subjects for fiction, and when they do, the result is often determinedly comic, as in work by Philip Larkin, John Betjeman, and Kingsley Amis. There are, of course, examples, like Muriel Spark's sardonic *Memento Mori* (1959) in which Dame Lettie Colson is brutally killed by a burglar, or, more recently, Graham Swift's emotive *Last Orders* (1996), of more complicated portrayals of Britain's aged population. Barker shows that it is easy for the young to underestimate the old: in his first meeting with Liza, Stephen shrugs off an early impression that she reads his thoughts, deciding that the old lady is incapable of parody even when she so closely imitates his own official language. Only when he listens closely to Liza and becomes fascinated with her stories does she cease to be 'a case', and he become a visitor rather than a caseworker. In Barker's fiction, the elderly resonate with meaning in that they are frequently the more symbolic in her wide cast of characters. From Alice Bell to Liza and Geordie, the elderly combine to tell stories that will be lost with their generation's demise.

Liza's England is a feminized retelling of British history and society but it is different in style from other novels that have covered similar ground. Zoe Fairbairns's *Stand We At Last* (1983) spans the 1850s to the 1970s by following five generations of women, the collectivity implying the kind of sisterhood that Barker never seems entirely comfortable with, except at the level of critique. Margaret Forster's *Shadow Baby* (1996) includes an elderly woman protagonist, but she is more concerned with tracing her mother than seeing the events of a lifetime in socio-political context. In Penelope Lively's *Moon Tiger* (1987), a dying Claudia composes the past out of shards and swathes of memory and Lively combines first- with third-person narration in a postmodernist disquisition on time, regret, and aphasia.[4] Barker's novel is the more hard-hitting. For Liza the past has outstayed itself: unfashionably and in socialist language, she attributes moral and ethical meaning to past history, just when the heritage industry had begun to package the past, developing it into a leisure industry that would withstand the onslaught of the millennium. Mining museums were erected in the 1980s on former coalfields, and visitors' centres stood beside the façades of what had formerly been functioning factories. The past could be reprised as educational entertainment. Barker sets Liza against this propensity and for Margaretta Jolly this forms part of the novel's challenge to 'the fragmentation of both post-industrial society and post-modern style'. It is also a recognition that, as Patricia Waugh reminds us, identity for marginalized persons is always constructed ideologically through 'impersonal and social relations of power' rather than as 'the reflection of inner "essence" '.[5] Liza's character is unravelled across the novel as a figure living in the interstices of past and present, of public and private history. Liza builds her themes into what Peter Hitchcock, deploying Mikhail Bakhtin's idea of the 'chronotope', has called 'community memory'.[6] It should, however, be noted that much of the story she tells is about how little people understand of one another and how they often fail to find the words to support each other.

Far removed from the euphemisms of the heritage industry is the underclass Barker explores in *Liza's England*, the boys like Whitey, Zit, and Scrubber on the Clagg Lane housing estate where the disaffected young hang about the streets. These are some of Stephen's charges. On this 'sink estate' the boys with whom Stephen comes into contact demonstrate the lowest levels of ambition and have only long-term unemployment and petty crime on which to plot their futures. They are cast adrift in contemporary society. One is reminded of the 'submerged tenth' of Victorian Britain but also of recent literary projects like Tony Harrison's vituperative *V. and Other Poems* (1990) in which an angry young skinhead decries:

> Folk on t' fucking dole
> 'ave got about as much scope to aspire
> above the shit they're dumped in, cunt,
> as coal aspires to be chucked on t' fucking fire.[7]

Barker carefully overlays one century with the next and elucidates the failings of one decade via another, an idea she pursues in more precise ways in *Another World*. The angry young men who finally leave Liza for dead having ransacked her home are unable to follow their fathers into the shipbuilding or steel-making industries. They have forestalled all sense of community except for their own twisted camaraderie. But the salient point Barker would draw our attention to is that 'in isolated pockets of total depression, people turn on each other'.[8] Set against these boys, Stephen figures as an extension of Liza. But Stephen is older, educated, and gay. As a carrier of hope for the future, he is untypical in the novel and very much alone.

Through Liza, Barker provides a kind of deep x-ray of the way life was lived in urban poverty in the north-east of England, and the mapping of her memories is 'chronotopic' in that the connectedness between space and time becomes apparent as the story is told. Liza's memories transcend simple chronology; they shift according to the meanings that Liza invests in them, as when she remembers a day of contentment spent with her brother Edward and revises that memory when it is juxtaposed with the desolate day she heard of his death (*LE* 50). Remembering dominates Liza's last year of life. Writer William Maxwell confides that, in old age, remembering can govern one's life and ruin a night's sleep: 'Before I can stop myself, it is as if I had driven a mineshaft down through layers and layers of the past and must explore, relive, remember, reconsider, until daylight delivers me.'[9]

However, Liza tries to organize her memories in an effort to meet and face both the past and her impending death. In this she is largely successful. Where she is, inevitably, ineffectual is in imparting her hard-won wisdom in a way that will help those who follow; what she has learned of life will be lost, just as her home is bulldozed immediately following her death. Like Alice Bell, who realizes that in the 1970s she is 'worse housed' than she was during the Depression (*US* 242), Liza is a pragmatist. She tries to be clear-sighted about life and what one may expect of it, but, again like Alice Bell, Liza is subject to her fears. Her greatest fear is the workhouse where her husband died: even decades after his death, the place retains a tenacious hold on her imagination because she fears the stigma of ending her life as a social cast-off. Whereas in *Another World* Geordie's memory sticks on a particular traumatic moment during the First World War, Liza floats back over a life that only Stephen begins to appreciate. He does so because he harbours a social worker's sense of lost agency and social declension and because his quiet safely guarded disaffection is punctured by his affection for this particular elderly lady.

SELF AT WAR

War cuts through *Liza's England*: the First World War slices Liza's life in two and her personal dilemmas are described as part of wider cultural transformations that include war and warfare. Liza, a mother and carer, is also a worker. Barker points up the division of labour through her war work on the assembly line, a gendered form of labour she paid particular attention to in *Union Street* and *Blow Your House Down*. In this novel, Barker returns to the assembly line and to the war economy that brought women into paid industrial employment during both wars. Sarah, who in *Regeneration* walks proudly through Edinburgh, her skin yellowed from sulphur, is one of the 'canary girls' we also see represented in *Liza's England* (*LE* 51). We begin to gain a sense of the history of light industry and the generally underexamined idea industrialists had that women might be more suitable than men to the monotonous routine of assembly-line work.[10] In the earlier novels it becomes apparent that women characters have spent years operating at the same pace in the same spot on the factory floor with no prospects of training, promotion, or change, and without the most basic of civil rights, even when pregnant. In *Liza's England*, there is a strong sense of women in a labour continuum with peaks at times of war, when their work is singled out as meaningful, and troughs when, post-war, they are re-established as mothers and domestic workers.

Ellen who works as a maid for the wealthy Wynyard family before the war draws attention to the ways in which class antagonism fuels the already problematic interdependence of women and war work. Elizabeth Wynyard is 'playing at work', according to her former maid. She feels strongly that her labour in the Wynyard home always remained unacknow-ledged so refuses to acknowledge Elizabeth's war effort: ''But she doesn't see us . . . She looks at you but her eyes never quite focus. She's not used to seeing people . . . I didn't exist at all' (*LE* 56). The non-seeing of those who serve is a motif that runs through the novel. As a cleaner for the Wynyard family before the war, Liza's mother Louise knows that 'You go round the back' (*LE* 29) and 'You're not supposed to be seen' (*LE* 34). She warns her daughter not to 'do anything to show us up' (*LE* 29), but Liza never chooses to learn the lessons her mother tries to teach about knowing one's place and resenting it. Louise is entrenched in resentment, 'Some so-called *ladies*'d be sat in their own muck like loonies if they didn't have us to run round after them' (*LE* 34). Liza may feel uncomfortable breaching class barriers (pulling out the cash and change she has saved to buy her granddaughter's grammar school uniform in a depart-ment store), but she rarely fades into the background. War is a constant source of fear and torment for women whose men go to fight. When Liza holds baby Tom just days after his birth, she is sharply aware that: 'They could take him away and kill him for no reason she would ever understand. They could fill his head with dreams of adventure and glory and make him want to go. Her son was no different from the rest' (*LE* 82).

Liza's relationship with her son is heightened by war. More generally, it would seem to echo Mrs Morel's with Paul in *Sons and Lovers* (1916), and remind us of Lawrence's examination in *Fantasia of the Unconscious* (1922) of a child caught between battling parents. There is, for example, what has been read as a typically 'Lawrentian' scene in which Frank, Liza's husband, cuts Tom's hair in a coming-of-age ritual. However, to call Barker Lawrentian is to damn her with faint praise: it is rather too simple to suppose such scenes are 'blatant lifts', as Michael Ross does before demonstrating the ways in which Barker 'creatively re-imagines' Lawrentian episodes.[11] Deifying Lawrence, one forgets that the scenes he described were archetypal working-class rituals. For Barker, a scene like the haircutting she describes is 'a story that is in every working-class family of that time. It wasn't written in dialogue with Lawrence, it was defiance, as if to say "I'm going to use this because this is a part of common territory"' (AI). Barker pays astute attention to what is common territory in twentieth-century British experience and reminds readers that the self at war is a fundamental experience that has marked more than one generation of Britons.

In *Liza's England* the soldier's experience is told through Liza's husband, Frank Wright. Like Septimus Smith in Virginia Woolf's *Mrs Dalloway* (1925), Frank imagines people are 'treading on dead faces', the faces of his dead comrades-in-arms. The prosperous who made money from warfare and the oblivious who let it pass over them – both of whom he resents – fail to see the faces of the dead, while Frank is alienated by what he has seen and cannot forget. Frank, more than any other character, is made and broken by war. Memories of war block his ability to live another life when he returns home. He dreams of rotting corpses on a blank, desolate wasteland across which men inch their way through mud. Frank 'died' once before in No Man's Land, where he lay for three days unwilling to return from the dead. He has an exceptional and highly visual memory of war:

> On either side of the track were shell-holes full of water and in one of them a trapped moon stared at the sky. Nothing moved except the line of men, shuffling forward. No trees, no grass, and the water that looked so pure would blister the skin that touched it. A film of grease floated on its surface ... (*LE* 82)

35

Frank's memory is presented as 'exceptional' in the way that Ian Hunter has assessed First World War veteran Alexander Aitken's memories, studied for their range, tenacity, and precision.[12] However, Frank is also subject to the same 'gusts of depression' that military psychologist W. H. R. Rivers has described as occurring in soldiers who fail to recall dreadful events that they have repressed.[13] Frank is tortured by the sheer, overwhelming detail of what he remembers to the extent that he considers suicide.

For Frank, the road to salvation is hard, but the motif of the resurrection, as powerfully evoked in a Renaissance painting by Piero della Francesca (1420–92), provides some consolation. Frank fixes on the painting *Resurrezione* as coming closest to his own tortured vision of death in life. Instead of a benign, beatified Christ, the face of the pale, emaciated man holding his flag of victory is resigned and battle-weary. His eyes stare out of the painting as if in shock and beneath him four guards lie sleeping in a slumber that resembles death. Reminiscent of Masaccio's composition in the famous painting *Trinità*, Piero della Francesca's *Resurrezione* shows the gap between the human and the divine. The question of perspective so important to Renaissance painters is brought home to Frank, for whom there can be no return to ordinary life following the war. In the painting and through the painter's eye, Frank finds a connection: 'Finding this picture was the most important event in his life, though he told nobody. Somebody else *knew*. He was not alone' (*LE* 87). Like Maggie at the close of *Blow Your House Down*, Frank seeks 'some revelation of good to balance the evil'. Maggie finds her thoughts drift back to 'the chicken Christ on the cross' – a painting tucked at the back of a country church because it is ugly. Frank feels 'set apart from other men' but he recognizes himself in their death. The pressure from the war wound in his throat is compounded by the pressure he feels to name the litany of the dead, to chant their names over and over like a catechism: '*Speak for us*, they said. *We cannot speak*' (*LE* 84).

Peter Hitchcock, following Liza's censure of Frank for being a 'parrot' rather than a conduit, believes Frank is a false historian, fraudulent because he fails to recognize any social context outside the personal connection to the men he knew in war and his grief over their deaths. It is certainly the case that war is personalized and that it produces the aesthetic experience of art for Frank. Despite the impact of della Francesca, whom Barker refers to directly, Frank's experience would seem to be best embodied by an English painter who was strongly influenced by Massaccio and Giotto and other Renaissance painters. Like Frank, Stanley Spencer was one of the few who returned to take up the life he had lived before the First World War. Private Spencer, a medical orderly, returned to Burghclere near Newbury in Berkshire to record the daily life of soldiers as art. His most famous painting, *The Resurrection of the Soldiers*, dominates the chapel at Burghclere. Spencer's coordinates of war, death, and Christianity are the same preoccupations that charge Frank's every word in *Liza's England*. Murals like *Reveille* and *Dug-Out*, which are included among Spencer's work in the chapel, were originally commissioned by the Berends family. Their son George remembers that 'ordinary people in the 1920s were shocked by Spencer'.[14] In Frank, too, the propensity to shock or unnerve those who have not experienced war sets him apart. Frank never reconciles himself to family life. Liza and Frank fail to communicate once she becomes a mother and he a spiritualist. It is Frank's alignment with Christ (he feels he is 'hidden with Christ in God') that leaves him forever at odds with the more secular Liza; their dissonance is epitomized in the exchange where Frank avers, 'God doesn't lay more burdens on us than we can carry' and Liza sharply retorts, 'Arseholes' (*LE* 91).

A STILTED CONVERSATION

Failure to communicate effectively is a significant theme for Barker. As one reads her novels, it becomes clear that there is a particular signature scene that unsettles the reader, a conversation, usually between men, that is attempted over and over but never fully realized. In *Liza's England*, it is expressed in the tacit unspoken affection between Stephen and his dying father. Their attempts at conversation are thwarted by their own awkward and frustrated resentments, 'They sat, father and son, facing each other across the hearth like a pair of electric plugs that wouldn't fit into each other . . .' (*LE* 39–40). It takes the intervention of Stephen's mother in a role she has played throughout his life temporarily to fuse the connection between them, but Stephen continues to feel they are 'light years' apart. In this case, as in many others that Barker explores across the novels, it is the difference in status that drives a class wedge between the men: the educated son has choices the father never knew nor could have had, as with Richard Scaife and his dying father in *Union Street*. But it is also the pressure of traditionally masculine stereotypes that makes them fumble their way around each other. On the night he dies, Walter tries to confide in his son that in later life he has been drawn to watching schoolgirls, finding himself passing a local school more and more regularly. Whilst for Walter the context is both confessional and a botched attempt to find some masculine common ground, Stephen finds the burden of his father's sexual desires inappropriate and the confession jars with his own homosexual identity about which he has remained silent. The men remain isolated. More generally, conversation is distinguished by a stilted formality, 'a few stiff sentences about the weather, then football, suitable topics' (*LE* 102). It is in this novel that Barker explores what will become a key trope in later fiction. When men like Billy Prior or Geordie Lucas are expected to express their emotions, it is like stepping on to 'untried ground' or into 'marshy, shifting unstable waters' (*LE* 114). Frequently, conversations between men fail to emote because of social conditioning, as army psychologist W. H. R. Rivers describes in *Regeneration*.

When questioned about scenes of fractured conversation, Barker agrees that 'the more difficult the speech is, the more powerful the background silence has got to be' (AI). She admits that she 'hears' the background silence more often between men than between women, but is adamant that this is not to say that women speak with more meaning simply because they may talk more easily. When Liza asks her elderly mother whether she ever loved her, Louise simply answers that she did not. If Louise expects anything it all, it is that, having lost a child herself, Liza will understand her mother's unwillingness to pour her emotions into her children: 'life caught up with me and I stopped trying' (*LE* 182). As early as *Union Street* Barker was exposing the fragility of the home and of familial relationships and more than once Liza fails to find words to express the 'stone-breaking struggle' of simply trying to manage a family in war and in poverty. She seeks 'words powerful enough to ignite the silence that was densely packed in her' (*LE* 167) and finally finds those words in old age, recounting for Stephen the life she has led as bound up with so many other lives.

The unpredictability of speech fascinates Barker throughout the Trilogy, but Barker's description of speech impediments in wartime begins with Frank, whose throat has been injured in war. On the one hand, he is presented as a showman-ventriloquist, in the opinion of a jaded Liza, but, on the other, he can also be read as a performance artist whose artistry lies in 'resurrecting' those silenced in death for their grieving mothers. Frank's throat is damaged, but he garners strength from 'speaking in tongues': the words of the fallen issue forth to sound the knell for a generation lost in war, 'mouths, silent, mud-stopped, gaped open and spoke' (*LE* 61). Without Frank as medium and message, his comrades-in-arms are locked into silence. Silence is a key metaphor in the text, as Jenny Newman explains. It can be a negative or positive force.[15] In the Regeneration Trilogy Barker explores how silence – mutism in war – can function as a form of protest, but in *Liza's England* silence is debilitating. The image of the 'blocked tongue', for example, attaches to a number of characters: following his father's death Stephen feels his silence 'impacted' in his throat; he drops his personal effects on leaving the hospital and discovers that Walter's slipper – like the broken shoes in which Louise trudged to work in the 1930s – has a sole that flaps 'like a tongue' (*LE* 123). Walter dies when a blood clot cuts off air and all powers of speech and Liza finally talks to Frank honestly as she washes his dead body. Louise recites the names of her dead children as she dies but remains silent about those children who surround her deathbed. Stephen imagines an intense, impassioned conversation he would like to have with his father, but Barker leaves it in his imagination; he has to play both parts.

BEATING TIME

Before he dies Walter impresses on his son that

> 'People don't know about time when they're working, it's all neat and tidy for them. You talk about passing time, killing time, and you don't know what you're on about. You don't kill time, time kills you. It gets your head like a pair of nut crackers and *squeezes*. Some afternoons I used to look at the clock, and I swear it didn't move.' (*LE* 117)

When Liza dies the clock on the mantlepiece is ticking, but 'a louder ticking had started inside of her. She beat time, not with her hands and her mind alone, but with every cell of her body' (*LE* 276). The act of her dying induces a kind of peristalsis in which time pulses to the surface. Later, in *Another World*, Barker describes 101-year-old Geordie living 'to the tick of a different clock' (*AW* 148). Frank Wright never escapes the nightmares of war, 'a white hand, moist, damp and cold, like a pad soaked in chloroform, came down over his face and pushed him down into the nightmares' (*LE* 82). The dreadful dreams are visceral: Frank can taste the nightmare on his tongue like bile, and even warming his hands on a mug of tea transports him back to similar times in the trenches. In death Barker's characters break out of the present and return to past times that were formative. Past history is how the elderly explain themselves to themselves – and to those who follow. However, with their deaths the reader is left feeling the future is uncertain. When Liza's house is finally demolished after her violent death, the waste ground where her street once stood is crossed with long black scars. Liza's possessions, 'the harvest of sixty years' hard labour', are 'junk' cleared out by a removal firm. Her erstwhile daughter Eileen pays a flying visit after her death, and the granddaughter Liza raised, one of Barker's few 'escapers' via college and university, is never mentioned. None of the youths whose careless cruelty precipitated her death is charged and Stephen is left quietly reeling from the shock. He is left to process the stories of the past that Liza left in his keeping, but he remains uncertain: after his father's death, he was left 'testing the worth of what was left' (*LE* 174) and after Liza's death, he feels that 'whatever had happened would reveal itself more fully in time' (*LE* 278), as the twentieth century has been revealed across this novel. There is a crisis in history, as Fredric Jameson has argued,[16] whereby an amnesiac postmodern culture fails to access the past, or to synthesize its lessons for the present. This is a contemporary problem that Pat Barker explores in the novels that follow *Liza's England*.

4

Performing the Self: *The Man Who Wasn't There*

> Knowledge and reason only play a limited part in a child's life. Its interest quickly turns away from the real things in the outer world, especially when they are unpleasant, and reverts back to its own childish interests, to its toys, its games and to its fantasies.
>
> (Anna Freud, *War and Children*, 1943)

LIVING IN ANOTHER WORLD

The Man Who Wasn't There takes place in September 1955 over three days in the life of 12-year-old Colin Harper. Colin lives in a community of women, including most notably his mother, Viv, who in her general dismissiveness of her son refuses to tell him anything at all about his father. It is this absence in the boy's life that Barker fills with Colin's imaginings. He loses himself in reveries usually set in wartime, in the year of his birth, 1943, in which he lives with 'one eye open for snipers'. Where Viv has fed Colin scenes from war films as spurious memories of his father, he creates the textual weave in which fiction and his quotidian reality become inextricably enmeshed. A mysterious 'man in black' enters and crosses over into his 'real' life saving Colin from an oncoming car as he daydreams his way across a road. The man recedes into the distance. The 'man who wasn't there' is Colin's projection of his absent father combined with his future self, or what Barker describes as 'a real emanation of his potential' (AI). The boy's expressive psychological state develops into a performance of selfhood that may help to engineer a way to unravel his future.

Colin lives in a dream world, but he is nothing like Billy Fisher, the archetypal hero of Keith Waterhouse's *Billy Liar* (1959), the northern working-class hero with his sights firmly set on London. Billy lives in an imaginary country, Ambrosia, where he is Prime Minister. Colin is a marginal, melancholic figure, despite his self-sufficiency on the streets of the north-eastern seaside town where he lives. He is an unsettled child, afraid of the dark, and in trouble at school for lateness and inattention. The other world he imagines counters but does not compensate for his unsettled present. In many ways, he may remind the reader of Kelly Brown, another child who seems more at home on the streets than in the family home, and Barker allows that he is pivotal in her writing: 'Colin at various stages of his life turns up quite often. When I was writing *Union Street*, the little boy Richard Scaife was a precursor for Colin. In the first draft he became a viewpoint character who functioned as a sort of identifier, like some of the characters in early plays by Dennis Potter: the character who is working-class but about to soar out of this narrow substratum of life so the middle-class reader can hope he gets to university soon!' (AI).[1] But Barker decided the boy's viewpoint would have been out of place in her first novel, as did Angela Carter, who read an early draft. Instead, Barker largely forgoes the 'escaper' as a type. In *The Man Who Wasn't There* Colin is a 'scholarship boy' but also a 'son of war', and an artist-in-the-making who is visually dominant and whose fantasy is a process of self-making. It is only later that his character mutates into the more disturbed and disturbing Gareth in *Another World*. Gareth, who creates an alternative wartime world in the computer battle zone of 'Streetfighter', seeks adventure but is dangerously out of touch with himself and reality.

If we follow Sigmund Freud, the process of individuation that any young boy undergoes rests on his identification with the father. The father figure represents abstractions like desire and independence, but the boy's autonomy and agency are learned from the father and defined as separation from the mother. To be without a father is to be caught up in an anxious search for a familial past and some way of asserting one's self as separate and distinctive from others. Colin is locked into revealing a past that he has access to but no experience of: 'For Colin, the mystery of his father's identity was bound up with the war, the war he'd been born into but couldn't remember' (*MWWT* 32). The imperative to remember that which cannot be remembered persists across the novel: in playground games in which schoolboys fight the war over and over each break time; in an evening's play on bomb sites in which the boys are bomber pilots, Dambusters, and victims rolling on the ground and screaming; and in the films from which Colin gleans most of his images of war.

But Freud also reminds us that we never invent by accident. 'Memory' in this novel is a simulacrum for a deep-rooted emotional response to loss. According to Viv, Colin's father was 'shot down', she attributes him a hero's death in the manner of *The Way to the Stars* (1945) with its paean to 'Johnny in the Clouds', the whole played to effect by Michael Redgrave, Rosamund John, and Douglas Montgomery. His father could be Michael Redgrave, or even Van Johnson in *Miracle in the Rain* (1955) – Colin admits that films become jumbled in his head. Hollywood teaches him that such men are brave. Colin seeks out heroism and believes in its images. In this way, the novel provides a disquisition on heroism and hero-worship. However, Barker ensures that masculine identity is a much more complicated site of enquiry than classical Hollywood allows. Barker asks what it might mean for a young fatherless boy to believe his father a hero; what it means when he sees through his mother's romanticization and self-deception, and what the effects might be when those precious, if spurious, images of heroism are transferred into his own life. When he finally realizes that films tell lies, 'they said it was easy to be brave' (*MWWT* 151), he learns a lesson that Barker tells with searing realism in the Trilogy that follows, where soldiers like Burns have 'missed [their] chance of being ordinary', since extreme situations and injuries become the norm in a war zone (*R.* 184). Masculine myths are crippled by actual war.

However, in *The Man Who Wasn't There* Colin creates a romance adventure in his head that has little sense of the horror of war. He sets it in France in a resistance cell, a place that exists on celluloid or in his imagination so he has little sense of the real pressures on resistance fighters tortured for information. The scenes Colin creates fail to transcend his own limited experience: the French citizens queuing at a Gestapo checkpoint include 'several schoolboys – wearing the maroon-and-gold blazer of Queen Elizabeth's Grammar School' (*MWWT* 17). His only research extraneous to the movies involves finding indecipherable papers in his mother's wardrobe and these prompt a plot centred on espionage and codes only spies can decipher. For Colin, suspense is the key and this he relishes; each vignette is suspended and rerun like a soap opera or dramatic serial, just as a child plays out the plot of a favourite movie over and over. The story Colin imagines is anti-realist and unintentionally comic in ways that reflect his age and unworldliness. Barker has him create melodrama and she invents a comic narrative-within-a-narrative in which scenes are sutured together in one of her most experimental novels. Barker writes a film screenplay, which she decants into the novel. But she also creates two distinct personae with the one life lived in parentheses. The two narratives are rendered differently, inscribing two different levels of reality, which, as Italo Calvino notes in his essay 'Levels of Reality in Literature', may be 'matched by different levels of credibility – or to put it better, a different suspension of disbelief'.[2] Calvino warns readers not to confuse levels of reality within the literary work with levels of truth outside it. Barker presents one story framed by another, so that her protagonist Colin Harper exists liminally in the text. Part of his personality is 'split off' or projected and it is this part that exists in cinematic form.

NOVEL AS SCREENPLAY

In a novel partly written as screenplay, the juxtaposition of images and the short chapters/scenes operate according to the principle of editing we understand from the cinema. Film is a kinetic, dynamic form and Colin's 'borrowings' from Holly-wood cinema ensure that he produces a classical Hollywood narrative but one told as a sequence of stressful events or scenes. Despite the space between scenes, Colin 'directs' his film 'in the can'. That is to say, he follows the process of continuity editing favoured by Hollywood that minimizes the shift from one scene to the next. But he never moves beyond the assembly stage by refining it to a 'final cut'. Editing is fundamental to the construction and generation of meaning in a film text. Colin edits in order to savour for himself the pleasurable experience of participating vicariously in a strange and dangerous world. In each scene Colin's alter ego is anxious, threatened, or frightened, many of the emotions the average cinema-goer craves. At one point he feels vulnerable but almost deliciously exposed, 'as if a layer of skin had been stripped from his back' (*MWWT* 57). In fact, Colin's 'other' life satisfies his requirements as an avid consumer of cinema. During the 1950s, when this novel is set, F. R. Leavis, a Cambridge don, famously argued that young people should be protected from what he believed to be the corrupting influence of cinema. This general feeling did not begin to be superseded for educators until the Newsom Report of 1963, which allowed for the incorporation of mass media studies into school curricula. For Colin in 1955, cinema is an environmental factor that helps to define his fears and desires.[3] It sharpens his visual and dramatic sense as a storyteller, but he is not a critical reader of his film-going experience.

For this 12-year-old boy, films are personally meaningful not ideologically loaded and he carefully selects a cast for his very own war story, which he writes, directs and edits only according to his own limited experience. He is Gaston, an orphan according to his identity papers, Von Strohm, the arch-villain Gestapo officer, is 'in another time and place' his headmaster, and his mother is Vivienne, a waitress/prostitute who dies in her son's story. Colin's immediate empirical world is spliced with the imaginary. The presentation of birth certificates on admission to school becomes a dangerous Gestapo checkpoint he has to get through, since his certificate is the 'short' version belying the fact that no father is stated. Before dispatching his mother's married boyfriend by telling him she expects marriage, he 'transforms' him into a Kommandant and then decides that a spiv is actually more in keeping. When Colin ignores the bullying a fat boy suffers at school, his alter ego Gaston becomes a traitor who plots to give up the names of others in his resistance cell (*MWWT* 79–84).

Colin generally reverts to his fantasies when confronted with fear or apprehension. The associations that trigger his perform-ance are often sensory, as when he lies in his 'favourite place', a bomb crater that has not been filled in. As he lies there, smelling dusty nettles, he becomes aware of 'other life here, small animals that darted and burrowed', and immediately drifts back to his life on celluloid (*MWWT* 123). He could be said to be involved in a mirror exercise of the type Constantin Stanislavski used in acting workshops to promote naturalistic performance. The actor 'becomes' the character. Stanislavski's emphasis on psychological realism was based on the idea that each aspect of the imaginary world the actor creates on stage – and in his head – must be real.[4] Breaking through the distance between the actor and his role took on progressively Freudian overtones down the twentieth century, an affective response to emotional 'memory' as 'Method acting'. But, while Liza in *Liza's England* has a box filled with props to prompt her memories, Colin's fantasy world is so real that it is expressive of his estrangement from the empirical world. It signals his dissatisfaction with what his life entails.

GENDER MODELS

A network of images derived from cinematic performance delivers the war safely as story in this novel, where the story is the passage between the real and the imagined (the present and an imagined past). War, its conflicts, effects, and emotional scars, is the ostensible subject of *The Man Who Wasn't There*, but Colin fails to apprehend it outside the bomb sites where he plays or the stories that proliferate in his post-war environ-ment. In fact, in *Border Crossing* set in the 1990s, boys play a game of war that has hardly altered at all, 'setting fire to enemy buildings' and 'living off the land' (*BC* 210). In *The Man Who Wasn't There* it is the cult of compulsory masculinity that is really examined and found wanting. If the novel is read as a search for role models with whom Colin might identify on the post-war domestic front, it is both comic and filled with pathos. Barker ensures Colin encounters varying examples of masculinity: neighbour Adrian, who fulfils the role of older brother; Viv's married boyfriend Reg, who refers to Colin as 'Sonny Jim' and becomes a Gestapo Officer in his 'other world'; Roy Rogers at the Gaumont cinema. Closer in age are the older boys he worships from a distance:

> Boys with braying laughs and sudden, falsetto giggles, boys who stood on street corners and watched girls walk past, who punched each other with painful tenderness, who cultivated small moustaches that broke down, when shaved, into crusts of acne thicker than the moustache had ever been, who lit cigarettes behind cupped hands, narrowing their eyes in pretended indifference to the smoke. (*MWWT* 28)

Barker captures the fragility of a young boy's ego and his yearning to identify with others in a masculine continuum. Most unsettling for Colin in this context is Bernie Walters, sweetshop owner and transvestite, who in a deep baritone tells Colin to 'piss off, sonny' (*MWWT* 34). When a teacher impresses on Colin the need for a male influence 'to ensure that a boy's development is . . . healthy', he weaves Bernie into his story as Bernard the Englishman. Bernard 'never had a father . . . no *male* influence. Nothing *healthy*. Nothing *normal* . . . never even joined the boy scouts' and takes to wearing his sister's knickers (*MWWT* 68–71). The words that Barker italicizes here map the contours of the terrain that Colin must occupy in order to begin to find his place. However, Colin never finds himself in safe territory in the story he concocts. His personality is not fixed but fluid and it is possible for him to lose sight of the coordinates of masculine identity that society finds the most comfortable. Colin is subject to the plethora of clichés around homosexual panic, as in his portrayal of Bernard. His tacit understanding of homosexuality underpins the character he imagines in ways that reflect those fictions of empire in which homosexuals were constructed as potential traitors who could be led to value sexual favours over patriotism.[5] In *Regeneration* W. H. R. Rivers bitingly compares 'The Great Adventure', the umbrella term for the stories boys devour, with the reality of a war that 'consisted of crouching in a dugout, waiting to be killed' (*R.* 107). Rivers gives the lie to the 'Adventure'; 'manly' activity has become passivity, while Colin's imaginary action-packed world remains the stuff of tenacious cliché as fortified by classical Hollywood.

A significant facet of the novel, also favoured by Hollywood, in films like *Tender Comrade* (1943) and *Ladies Courageous* (1944), is the depiction of women who relished the freedom of the Home Front. They are 'out of the cage', to borrow a phrase repeated by so many women interviewed about their war work.[6] Colin's mother and her friend Pauline reminisce about their time in the Auxiliary Territorial Service (ATS), 'manning' anti-aircraft guns – though Winston Churchill had forbidden women from actually firing them. Pauline is wistful: 'I think the first two years of war were the happiest of my life' (*MWWT* 102). Both women regret their loss of status in the workforce at the end of the war. Barker looks seriously at the role of women in war, a topic she develops in more detail in the Trilogy. In *The Man Who Wasn't There*, there is also something of the vaude-villian in Barker's representation of Viv and Pauline. They waitress in a club dressed as fawns, a bizarre take on Hugh Heffner's equally bizarre idea that Bunny tails made his girls seem untouchable. Colin is expected to steam Viv's fawn ears each evening before she departs for work. Rather than lament leaving her young son to fend for himself, Viv is more worried that 'thirty-six was over the hill, for a fawn' (*MWWT* 36). Colin, understanding little of her desires or her loneliness, manages, like *Union Street*'s Kelly Brown, to frighten her boyfriends away with his childish precocity. Despite the pathos in the relationship, there is much salt at its edges. It often circles around sex: one young woman, Enid, becomes pregnant by the back end of a pantomime horse and is the talk of the town. Colin is privy to the gossip his mother and grandmother bring into the house about women and 'women's problems' and one character, Mr Stroud, is even described as 'a small, balding, sperm-shaped man' (*MWWT* 110). Much of Colin's self-doubt relates back to his adolescent fears about sex and sexuality and his desperate search for meaning in masculinity.

WRITING AGAINST THE GRAIN

A key issue that is made clear in *The Man Who Wasn't There* is Barker's preoccupation with the spiritual medium as a meta-phor for the artist and her fascination with the supernatural and ghosts, ideas she takes up in more detail in *Another World*. Barker domesticates the supernatural in her descriptions of the 'spuggies', the seances popular in a grieving post-war Britain. Mrs Stroud manufactures her 'second sight', but her routine is disturbed when she focuses on Colin and is able to 'see' a spirit at his shoulder and to detect in the boy untapped psychic powers, the powers that have driven his imagination through-out the novel. Ironically, it is precisely what is *real* about her role of medium that shocks a comfortable congregation out of the fraudulent routine she manages so successfully for them each session. Faking the real also highlights that which is not quite fake and reminds us that the real is always possible. In *Liza's England* Frank Wright knows when his power as a medium fails and he has to choose whether he will continue in a motivational role for those mourning parents who hang on his every word. In this novel, Mrs Stroud makes a living by giving her clients and neighbours the very advice they need from 'the other side'. She is more community counsellor than medium. Barker's literary exploration of therapy begins in interesting ways. In *Regeneration* Prior both is mute and fakes mutism and in *The Ghost Road* Barker has the spiritual medium in Melanesia show that he knows how to fake divination, 'he savvy gammon lang naasa'. Where the rational explanation does not fit the facts, Barker posits another version of the real, and it is in *The Man Who Wasn't There* that this key feature of her aesthetic vision really begins to come into play.

Barker often writes against the grain and against expecta-tions but perhaps not more so than in *The Man Who Wasn't There*, her fourth published work. One reason, one supposes, that this novel has failed to receive as much critical attention as her other works is that the surreal elements push the novel further outside the predominantly realistic framework of the earlier fiction. With a nod to Kafka, Barker has Viv tell her feverish son that when she had a high temperature as a child, 'I thought I was a cockroach. I could hear me wings rubbing together and everything' (*MWWT* 144). While Gaston fakes an illness, over the days in which the action take place Colin has become progressively ill until he faints and falls into a fever. When Gaston sees a dead Vivienne propped up on a chair next to her resistance colleagues, he panics and the scene fades out until Colin sees his mother seated in the very same chair in his bedroom talking him through his fever. Surrealism bleeds out of the film and into Colin's quotidian realm. The novel twists and turns on what may be 'real' and what 'fake'.

The novel has been subject to little critical reading and some misreadings. It has been under-read, as though a child protagonist relegates the fiction to a space outside Barker's best work. This is a pity, since this novel is a pivotal text in coming to understand many of the themes and ideas that circulate in Barker's fiction. Certain reviewers, like Herbert Mitgang in the *New York Times*, feel that father and son fuse in Colin's imagination.[7] But this is a surface recognition of only one role that Barker has Colin play. Discrepant or partial readings perhaps reflect Barker's own writing practice in this novel. She circles Colin: 'I knew at some point that Colin ... would have to face the man who wasn't there, but I didn't know it was himself. There was a point at which I thought it was a ghost and at one point I thought it was a prowler.'[8] The Freudian psychoanalyst Bruno Bettelheim in his discussion of fairy tales argues that, the less specific the writer is about the hero, the more readers empathize and endow him with their own meanings.[9] This idea holds true for *The Man Who Wasn't There*. Colin is unable to control the fiction he creates, no matter how carefully he scripts his story, and the reader feels his anxiety, the source of his creativity, as the dominant effect. While Barker refused to depict Colin as an uncomplicated 'scholarship boy' in the mould of Richard Hoggart's definition, Colin does reflect the more uneasy components of the type. For Hoggart, the 'scholarship boy' is always self-conscious and filled with self-doubt. This is especially true of Colin when one considers his anxious efforts to link two discrete environments he is coming to know – the 'men's world' he needs to feel he belongs to and the 'women's world' he knows best. Hoggart explains: 'With one ear he hears the women discussing their worries and ailments and hopes, and he tells them at intervals about his school and the work and what the master said. He usually receives boundless and uncomprehending sympathy: he knows they do not understand, but still he tells them; he would like to link the two environments.'[10] Much of Colin's ambivalent relationship with 'another world' reflects the exasperated hope of reconciling his own position when it conflicts with the traditional class and gender expectations of the community into which he has been born. It is an exasperation that Barker believes continues into adulthood – and one is reminded of the title of Richard Hoggart's collection of essays, *Between Two Worlds* (2001).[11] Towards the end of his 'film', Gaston/Colin has become a traitor, killed Vivienne/his mother, and imagined his father into being, but failed to link them. He conjures up an adult self far removed from his childhood setting. In one of the most moving scenes of the novel Colin watches his adult self return to the home he shares with his mother to attend her funeral, a traitor to his class and to his family. The 'man in black' – dressed for a funeral rather than espionage – wears Colin's face but seems to feel very little emotion. Colin rejects this cold, alien figure and in so doing kills off his alter ego Gaston. No longer believing himself to be solely the extension of an elusive father, but also deeply connected to a less-than-perfect but present mother, he lets the curtain fall on his acting apprenticeship for the last time. Out of a fragmented, volatile self, made and remade in performance and fantasy, he gains a sense of a more *integral* self.

unnecessary prolonging of battle in his public protest of 1917, 'A Soldier's Declaration', a statement that left him at the mercy of the war office, the press, and the military for some time. But he was also a courageous soldier who returned to fight at the Front. The quiddity of human nature encapsulated in Sassoon's personal and ethical quandary drives *Regeneration* and the Trilogy.

Barker begins in a very specific historical context, Craig-lockart War Hospital over a few months in 1917, and through specific relationships like Sassoon's with W. H. R. Rivers, the military psychologist. She begins to translate large abstractions about patriotism and pacifism, courage and fear, into encounters between individual characters. At first sight this technique might be understood as a nod to liberal humanist ideas in which the individual conscience and attendant behaviour dominate. In fact, Barker recognizes that, in approaching such a hugely emotive subject, it is more difficult to mourn faceless millions of war dead than a single person whom one comes to 'know'. When Barker visited First World War grave sites in France for the BBC documentary *On the Ghost Road* she said, 'Once you find and identify a name that is known to you, it opens the past in a different kind of way.'[2]

The Great War has been mythologized largely through what we have come to call the literature of memory. The interweaving of memoir with history, and fiction with factual accounts, characterizes works that explore the war from within their writers' memories, as Edmund Blunden's *Undertones of War* (1928), Richard Aldington's *Death of a Hero* (1929), and Robert Graves's *Goodbye To All That* (1929) have shown. This propensity is transformed down the century, so that historian Niall Ferguson begins his history *The Pity of War* (1999) with an account of his own grandfather's experience of the First World War and of the way in which monuments and memorials across Britain affected him in his youth. The Imperial War Museum estimated at the close of the twentieth century that there remained as many as 60,000 war memorials throughout Britain.[3] War-inspired fiction continues to proliferate, from Susan Hill's *Strange Meeting* (1971), influenced by Owen's poem of the same name and by Sassoon's 'Lamentations'; and Paul Bailey's *Old Soldiers* (1980), a novel about the persistence of memory in which two survivors of the Somme meet sixty years after the event; to Sebastian Faulks's acclaimed *Birdsong* (1993); and Melvyn Bragg's *The Soldier's Return* (1999), in which a working-class soldier is adjusting to home after the Second World War. Barker has referred to the First World War as a topic that is in danger of becoming 'overdone', but her own intervention into the subject provides the most sustained and challenging late-twentieth-century perspective on the First World War in literature. The Trilogy was published when the Gulf War dominated readers' reactions to the effects of war, through debates about Gulf War Syndrome, and so comments indirectly on contemporary conflict and the need to address society's expectations of combatants.[4] Barker animates what is abstruse about a war that almost no one now remembers first hand and breaks open some of the old myths about masculinity and bravery in war that persist and that have grown over old wounds like a new skin, too soon to allow proper examination.

Across the novels Barker has been said to monumentalize the Great War and its effects on British men and women, but this is easy rhetoric. She achieves much more and differently. Barker investigates the *effects* of memorializing and it is not finally to monuments that Barker turns: many of her most profound and painful concerns are inscribed on the bodies of the living. As we are told in *The Eye in the Door*, 'In the end moral and political truths have to be proved *on the body*, because this mass of nerve and muscle and blood is what we are' (*ED* 112). In the early novels, it is women's bodies that are under most stress: reproduction is the dominant role and risk for girls as for women and involves danger and distress. The men's bodies are strategically peripheral in the early texts, since unemployment leaves them ill at ease at home and lost on the streets. Their very existence as a labour force, as well as their roles, run the risk of extinction. In the later texts, where war is the focus, men's bodies are on the line, precariously situated at the interstices of war and nationhood.

SHELL SHOCK AND PSYCHIATRY

Regeneration is an exploration of the variegated forms of military psychiatry. It opens out a debate on methodology and ethics that historians have been trying to resolve across the twentieth century, in books by William Moore and Frank Richardson to more recent studies like Anthony Babbington's *Shell Shock* (1998) and Hans Binneveld's *From Shell Shock to Combat Stress* (1998). War neuroses and their diagnoses draw out difficult issues of morale and ideology. The propitious truths that Rivers teases out of his charges send them back to the Front and in symbolic exchange and reciprocity they are changed from psychiatric casualties to responsible soldiers – who must kill or be killed. Barker moves the aesthetic emphasis beyond the symbolic into the semiotic. Across the Trilogy terms like 'hysteria' and 'shell shock' are explored in their application and effect. Moffet, treated by Rivers in *The Ghost Road*, prefers 'shell shock', and Rivers understands the attraction of the more masculine term, even though it may be a misleading and inappropriate way to describe the hysteria from which his patients suffer. Since 'hysteria' derives etymologically from the Greek word for womb, it inhibits men for whom masculine endeavour and agency are the key to recovery, and for whom patriotic responsibility is synonymous with heroism. Barker sets up a clear contrast between Doctor Lewis Yealland's electric shock treatment, shocking patients whom hysteria has rendered speechless back into speech, with Rivers's cognition that symptoms and neuroses associated with shell shock are a kind of self-censorship. Mutism could displace the anger officers felt towards their superiors who controlled the attacks and provide a cover for their powerlessness to protest. Consequently, Sassoon's protest is all the more unusual a reaction and his return to France is often seen, by Elaine Showalter for instance, as defeat – defeat by therapy and by the framing of his anti-war protest as neurosis.[5]

Barker shows how dangerously easy it is to slip into homogenizing soldiers as cannon fodder when their responses to warfare are more wide-ranging than the ways psychologists and doctors find to treat them. Rivers's charges are those described in Owen's 'Mental Cases': 'men whose minds the Dead have ravished . . . Wading sloughs of flesh these helpless wander . . . always they must see these things and hear them.' Originally entitled 'The Deranged' and later 'The Aliens' and written in the summer of 1918, Owen's text speaks most clearly of Craiglockhart Hospital and comments ironically on the jingoism that promotes 'the old lie' about war and patriotism that Owen came to despise. Paul Fussell has noted the significance of irony as a tool for those who write about war. He believes that 'every war constitutes an irony of situation because its means are so melodramatically disproportionate to its presumed ends'.[6] A clear example might be Owen's editorial in the 17 September edition of the *Hydra*, Craiglock-hart's hospital magazine: 'In this excellent concentration camp we are fast recovering from the shock of coming to England. For some of us were not a little wounded by the apparent indifference of the public and the press, not indeed to our precious selves, but to the unimagined durances of the fit fellow in the line.'[7] He extrapolates on Sassoon's 'Declaration' in its bitter attack on public complacency and hones the irony for which the magazine became known. Meanings produced ironically are always implicit and past trauma may be crystal-lized in a moment: Prior retrieving Tower's eyeball from the wreckage of his body ('What am I supposed to do with this gob-stopper?'); Manning's memory of shooting Scudder in mercy for a sensitive soul blasted into a sand trap from which he could not extricate himself; and Burns who, upended by a bomb blast, realizes as he loses consciousness that he has landed on a blown-out corpse and is inhaling the suppurating body as he gasps for air. Burns's experience recalls the drawings of Otto Dix, and Prior's memory of men blundering around in gas masks recalls Owen's 'Dulce Et Decorum Est'. Such nightmare descriptions are attached to names and char-acters in the Trilogy and consequently personalized. Charac-ters like Prior, Burns, and Manning act as interlocutors for what is 'ungraspable' about their experiences 'out there'. Through their memories tranches of frontline quotidian horror are stripped bare.

There are certainly connections one might choose to make with Septimus Smith in Woolf's *Mrs Dalloway* (1925), an early literary version of Sassoon, which could be read as a significant influence, as could Chris Baldry in Rebecca West's *The Return of the Soldier* (1918) and Lord Peter Wimsey, who dominates so many of Dorothy L. Sayers's novels.[8] But easy equations between literary figures risk subsuming the established fact that many men, not only characters in novels, suffered from hypnagogic hallucinations of the kind that Septimus Smith and Barker's Sassoon experience. Barker makes this clear, especially since earlier, in *Liza's England*, she has Frank Wright a week out of hospital watching civilians treading on dead faces on the pavement. Many of her minor characters – including Harrington and Wansbeck in *The Ghost Road* – are riven with similar fears and paranoia. Army psychologist Rivers voices one of Barker's major concerns: 'There was a real danger, he thought, that in the end the stories would become one story, the voices blend into a single cry of pain' (*GR* 229). So, while drawing the reader into her exploration of war and its effects through figures we know – or have at least heard of – Barker refuses to make Sassoon or Owen representative.

Virginia Woolf's idea of 'tunnelling' as a narrative strategy that strikes a chord in connection with Barker. Woolf avowedly saw writing as 'dig[ging] caves' behind her characters.[9] Barker and Woolf are very different British writers, but the perspective they each bring to character is striking for the psychological depth they achieve. The penetration of a character's consciousness is seldom consolatory in either Woolf's or Barker's work. Instead, as soldiers cast back in time in search of memories, the capacity to live beyond the body, in symbol and nightmare, becomes achingly clear. Characters like Prior and Sassoon battle to keep their tortured memories under control; Sassoon shuts the lid on his and blinks terrifying thoughts away. When Prior begins to court Sarah Lumb and discovers that she makes detonators for the war effort, 'he thought what the detonators she made could do to flesh and bone and his mind bulged as memory threatened to surface' (*R.* 89). Characters twist and torque as they try to extricate themselves from thoughts that shut down their capacity to live beyond the war. Many of the characters in Barker's Trilogy survive by splitting off parts of themselves into dissociated consciousness: the part that kills or fears or desires houses the experiences that it is easier to repress. It is Rivers's task to uncover these repressed fears and to liberate the dual nature of the individuals in his care. This feature is particularly powerful in *The Eye in the Door*, the most angry of the three novels. In it Barker pushes to the limits of human psychological endurance, with Sassoon unable to stop talking about the vast incomprehensibility of war and Prior's 'other' dissociated self attending a consultation with Rivers in which he will only talk about 'Billy' in the third person.

In the process of the 'talking cure', Prior describes his alternate self: 'I was born two years ago. In a shell-hole in France. I have no father.' Perhaps more than any other statement, this epitomizes the intergenerational tension that results from passages in which definitions of the word 'generation' mutate. For Prior 'generation' becomes an exaggerated reference to his experience in the field, 'in trench time he was old. A generation lasted six months, less than that in the Somme, barely twelve weeks.' Prior thinks of himself as the great-grandfather of a new officer, Hallett, who is yet to experience the Front whilst he is returning for the fourth time (*GR* 46). Elaine Showalter argues in *Sexual Anarchy* (1990) that self-fathering has become a central myth of our times and we see its inception in the First World War. The Front becomes a zone of obligation for Sassoon and Owen and for Prior; it involves them in a tortured relationship with war based on responsibility for their men. When hospitalized with a head wound, Sassoon feels 'amputated' from his men, and, again, Barker's propensity to inscribe the mental pain of war on the male body is apparent in the disturbing metaphor.

THE FRONT AND THE HOME FRONT

Young men walked into the blanket fire and across the battlefields of Gallipoli, the Somme, Loos, Ypres, and Passchendaele and suffered what has since been described as the greatest loss of life in military history. Each battle was futile, in so far as trench warfare had protracted the struggle and men living like troglodytes in a war zone felt increasingly alienated from the Home Front, and from the decisions being made by those whose strategies purported to control the war zone. Conversely, the actual trenches Barker delays describing for so much of the Trilogy are everywhere at home. The trenches are themselves named after London streets, and Britain's urban landscapes, devastated by poverty and deprivation, are crystallized in the blasted terrain of the trenches. Prior describes the trench experience as 'a sort of *moral disgust*' with one's surroundings (*GR* 174) and, in *The Eye in the Door*, when he visits Beatie Roper in Aylesbury prison, the prison landings remind him of the trenches he has so recently left behind: 'No Man's Land seen through a periscope, an apparently empty landscape which in fact held thousands of men' (*ED* 30). Walking across Salford's brick fields, Barker has Prior fall into a trench dug by boys in a bizarre pastiche of war. The disorienting sense of the war's beginning in the heart of Prior's childhood past is a telling indictment of the English myth of a green and pleasant land and provides a painful context for his betrayal of Patrick MacDowell and the Roper family in *The Eye in the Door*. For Prior, the war becomes the nightmarish culmination of the life he has always led with the 'reduction of the individual to a cog in a machine'. He observes the expressions on the faces of men trapped at the front line, 'the rabbit-locked-up-with-a-stoat look', understood only because he remembers a family of boys from his childhood who had the same look because their father beat them every night, no matter how well behaved they might have been (*ED* 173–4).

Rudyard Kipling called the cemeteries housing white crosses marking the lost generation 'silent cities'. In *The Ghost Road*, Barker finally turns to the trenches that have been silently lying beneath the surface of her examination of the Home Front. The Trilogy ends on the Sambre-Oise canal, where Wilfred Owen met his end a week before the end of the war. Billy Prior, shadowing Owen, leads his men to their deaths: the angry young man of *Regeneration* has changed into a leader over the three novels, dying as he watches Owen die, ironically feeling his own life ebb away. The last days of the war were, for Barker, the most poignant and prolonged, when men were 'sacrificed to the sub clauses and the small print' of the Peace Treaty (*GR* 249). This is her most acrid disquisition on the waste of human life. Barker's most persistent character is dispatched by a single bullet and his death is juxtaposed with the long and painful death of a fellow officer, Hallett, in a London hospital under Rivers's care.

In the Trilogy the war becomes the unit of human movement and the basis for judging others. In January 1916, Prime

Minister Herbert Asquith introduced military conscription and the country was split. Those who registered as conscientious objectors were often imprisoned and some were killed, as Felicity Goodall has outlined in *A Question of Conscience* (1997).[10] By the end of the war, 16,000 men had registered and in *The Eye in the Door* Barker explores the ideas and ideals that motivated not only the well known like Bertrand Russell (who spent five months in jail after publishing *War: The Offspring of Fear* in 1914) or Lady Ottoline Morrell and Robert Ross, friends of Sassoon, but the ordinary men and women whose lives are wrung out when, like Beatie Roper in *The Eye in the Door*, they are vilified as criminally unpatriotic. Behind their stories lies the general awareness that men on the front line were frequently shot for 'cowardice', for leaving the ranks. The ideological stranglehold of patriotism and paranoia intrigues Barker. Beatie Roper is described by a prison warden as 'common as muck'. Both she and her son are psychologically weighed down by the 'eye in the door', the painted eye around the peephole in the cell door that forms its pupil. This is a nightmare image for Prior, whose most persistently repressed memory has been of discovering a comrade's eyeball in the debris of death around him in the trenches. Barker shows that, in the trenches and in the prison, soldiers and objectors are regulated by the same authoritarian system of surveillance made familiar through the metaphor of the Panopticon Michael Foucault uses to describe the oppressive watchfulness inherent in the prison system, even when physical violence is not an immediate threat: 'There is no need for arms, physical violence, material constraint. Just a gaze, a gaze which each individual under its weight will end by internalizing' until each individual becomes self-regulating.[11] The war is pervasive and invasive.

Barker makes clear what might otherwise seem opaque through the anti-war effort as explored in *The Eye in the Door*. Prior finds himself in the invidious position of working as a government spy for the Ministry of Munitions whilst troubled by his allegiance to the Roper family he is sent to investigate. But Prior is nothing like the spies in novels by John Le Carré or Graham Greene. Prior spent his childhood with the Roper family in Salford, and, when Barker takes him back to his northern roots (the kind of territory we know well from the early fiction), she has him take centre stage. Both Rivers and Sassoon appear, however. Rivers continues to treat Prior, who visits the older man at his home in Lancaster Gate in London, and Rivers maintains his contact with Sassoon. The connective tissue between these men remains. Rivers is the psychological glue that holds Barker's characters together and he comes to the fore when Prior begins to experience fugue states that interfere with his autonomy and present Barker with the opportunity to pursue the ethical conflict Prior feels about his job in Intelligence. Conspiracies of war resonate throughout *The Eye in the Door*. Prior is disgusted by Spragge, for example, a spy who is paid a bonus each time he 'brings in' an objector. But he is more disgusted by himself, so much so that his final betrayal of his childhood friend, Mac, is subsumed in one of his fugue states, the blank periods of which he has no obvious memory.

Beatie Roper's question, 'Whose side are you on?', is crucial. Barker shows us a divided country in which war propaganda has criminalized pacifists and socialists like Beatie and homosexuals like Charles Manning. Prior has affinities with each of these positions, which he largely batons down in order to remain competent at his job. The pressures of business and the guilt of betrayal rend him asunder and the result is a split personality. The epigraph to Robert Louis Stevenson's 1896 story *The Strange Case of Dr Jeckyll and Mr Hyde* provides a popular literary context through which readers apprehend the horror of Prior's situation. Characters like Prior who play on their internal divisions and those of others can be divisive. Prior turns in on himself and against the father physician, Rivers, in the role he outwardly performs. This duality is a fascinating feature of Barker's aesthetic in the Trilogy and elsewhere and one to which I shall return in the Postscript to this study.

WOMEN AT WAR

Barker touches on the role of women in war in earlier novels. In *Liza's England* Liza's daughter Eileen joins up while Liza suffers through the air raids at home, and in *The Man Who Wasn't There* women working in the ATS feel freed from the restrictions of their gender for once in their lives. The latter is a side effect of war that Barker returns to in the Trilogy. She notes at various points that the social space that women occupy has generally expanded, while the space that the men occupy has contracted into the trenches: the men have been 'mobilized into holes in the ground so constricted they could hardly move' (*R*. 107). The traditionally feminine passivity that Rivers notes while studying neurasthenic officers is contrasted with the working woman's new-found freedom. Sarah Lumb is liberated from domestic service when she takes up munitions work and receives a reasonable wage for the first time. However, as Karin Westman points out in her close reading of *Regeneration*, when women trespass on male territory, 'they are expected to be more masculine *and* feminine to succeed – and they must be willing to cede their new freedoms when the war is over'.[12] Sarah's mother remains persistent in her warnings that Sarah learn to use her sexuality to her advantage in order to make a good marriage; she is clearly sceptical that any change in gender politics could be permanent.

The insidious rift between men's and women's experiences of war stretches between them like a measureless wasteland. Prior positions his fiancé Sarah as a 'haven' (*R*. 216), since he need never explain to her what he has undergone in war. But he also uses her as an object on which to vent his anger, precisely *because* she can never understand what he has endured. Sarah and her friends are of strategic and symbolic importance. Women in the Trilogy are like the 'river daughters' in T. S. Eliot's *The Wasteland* (1922), but whereas in Eliot's story of Lil and Albert the woman always comes off worse, in *Regeneration* Lizzie tells Sarah that the day her husband went to war, '*Peace* broke out' (*R*. 110). Lizzie's husband is a domestic abuser and the war has released her from his fists. As Barker points out: 'In *The Wasteland* the women are used simply as caricatures of degeneration. I wanted to take that and use it in the opposite way, to make the women people who speak for life in this deadly world' (AI). Eliot had read Rivers's essays on Melanesia and Barker became interested in what she sees is an 'incredibly circular system of references' whereby motifs and images recur across a series of key texts (AI). She re-envisions Eliot's women characters so that they stand, like Rivers, as representatives of reasonable thinking (AI).

However, the women are also clearly much more than symbols. They are deeply involved in war work and some, like Beatie Roper and her daughter, are motivated and active participants in the politics of war. More generally, women are munitions workers, yellowed through contact with phosphorous, and still trapped by their ability to reproduce: one woman, Betty, uses a steel coathanger in a desperate, failed attempt to terminate her pregnancy (R. 202). The 'Munitionettes' produced 80 per cent of all weapons and shells by 1917, the year in which Barker sets *Regeneration*; women were killed in factory explosions and suffered the effects of working with dangerous chemicals. They earned less than those men undertaking the same work, but they also militated against the complacency soldiers detected in the populace.

CONFLICT AND ENCOUNTER

Barker is interested in those dramas that take place on the serrated edges of the military experience. Barker shows that the instruments of war are not only bombs, bullets, and bayonets but include the psychological pressure under which the doomed youths lived in the trenches and war hospitals. Barker also compared female support networks with men in the trenches long before she started work on the Trilogy and a salient problem she continues to raise is the difficulty of communicating across socially constructed boundaries.

Class relations were radicalized by the First World War and it was in 1918 that the Labour Party became a political force to be reckoned with. Rivers even stood as a Labour candidate, dying on the eve of the general elections in 1922. The politicization of the working classes had a peculiar impact on the nation. The triadic model of the upper, middle, and working classes begins to unravel on the Home Front during the war years. But it is the inflexible hierarchy within the military that so angers Prior. Barker provides only one example of 'men' and 'officers' coming together, to play street-corner football in the spirit of public-school rugby in No Man's Land (GR 173). Snobbery for Prior 'represents everything in England that isn't worth fighting for', and Barker has said that Billy Prior was 'a way for the two worlds to confront one another, rather than abandoning one and concentrating entirely on the other'.[13] In other words, Prior is the conduit between the classes. His resistance to class snobbery is important in terms of the weight Barker places on class analysis. In *The Ghost Road*, when Prior is stationed just outside Scarborough, he wanders out to the beaches and notes that 'you couldn't walk anywhere in Scarborough without seeing the English class system laid out before you in all its full intricate horror' (*GR* 34–5). The same bitter bile rises as he recalls for Rivers his anger at a Cambridge don's distaste for 'WCs' – the working classes.

In each encounter class relations are placed under the novelist's microscope. As an officer, it is Prior's responsibility to censor the letters the men send home and, in the sequence in which he reads and rereads snippets of men's lives, two class-bound societies are interwoven (*GR* 220–1). Prior is a hybrid character and an interlocutor for the men: in him 'officers' and 'men' may be combined but class distinctions remain inescapable. Class indelibly marks each relationship Barker explores. *The Eye in the Door* opens with Billy Prior studying the 'tight-lipped' rows of tulips on the banks of the Serpentine. He turns an imaginary machine gun on them and blasts them to bits. Shortly afterwards, following a botched liaison with a married woman, he is contemplating sex with the stiff-upper-lipped Charles Manning.

This particular encounter is illustrative of the close cross-class, cross-rank empathies that Barker creates out of a holocaust of suffering, but, as she points out, 'there's an awful lot going on between Manning and Prior which actually has nothing to do with sex but everything to do with the fabric of English society' (AI). George Bernard Shaw once observed that an Englishman need only speak to make another Englishman despise him and in this encounter Barker plays out the maxim to wry effect:

> Prior ran his fingers through his cropped hair till it stood up in spikes, lit a cigarette, rolled it in a particular way along his bottom lip, and smiled. He'd transformed himself into the sort of working-class boy Manning would think it was all right to fuck. A sort of seminal spittoon. And it worked. Manning's eyes grew dark as his pupils flared. (*ED* 11)

On the one hand, the upper-class house in which the men meet and the class system that regulates their day-to-day relations are resilient. On the other, Barker shows that the social fabric is damaged, shot through with flaws and faultlines that cross relationships. The house is Manning's family 'pile'; beneath the dustcovers are photographs of his wife and children. However, the house's foundations have been undermined by the bombing and the family stands on shaky ground. Prior has sidestepped into a situation where he takes control sexually. But Manning chooses where the sex should take place. The room in which the men have sex is the maid's quarters and Prior feels a shock of class recognition: when he breathes in the smell of the maid's uniform hanging in the closet, it is suffused with memories of his mother. Cleverly Barker entangles class expectations and cross-class transgressions in this sequence.

Cross-class encounters mediate into cross-cultural connections in *The Ghost Road* as Rivers's memories of Melanesian experience in the Baring Straits impinge more and more on his days and nights. Associations are initiated by sound (the click of a blind) or by sight (a ray of sun breaking through a closed curtain). Though Rivers bemoans the fact that he has little visual memory, in a high fever it returns. Each memory signifies a revelation and allows the reader to penetrate more closely reactions to war, death, and desire. Rivers's landlady has created a shrine to her dead son on the mantlepiece, much like the skull houses Rivers observed in Pa Na Gundel. His sister Katharine is confined to bed in later life, her adulthood cramped by domesticity since she has no recourse to a less confining, less 'feminine' home life.[14] Distinct patterns of war emerge in the novel: the Melanesians are perishing from the *absence* of war and Barker has said this is precisely what drew her to the topic: 'Rivers's sister and the woman whose mourning for a husband means reducing her world to the dimensions of a tiny box are mirror images of each other' (AI).

Within Barker's description of Rivers's anthropology there is a biting critique of colonialism through the nursery diseases carried by missionaries which prove fatal to the civilizations they visit themselves upon. But more telling, perhaps, is the implication of Rivers's own part in defining what is 'primitive' or 'pagan' against what is 'civilized'. As Barker juxtaposes

Rivers's memories of headhunters in the Baring Straits with the war experiences of Prior and others, Western paradigms are counterpointed with non-Western cosmology as the exploration of war expands across the Trilogy. As Prior departs for France, Rivers, having pronounced him fit to fight, is reminded of the Melanesian custom in which a father kills his adopted son. It is very like the Bible story of Abraham, who was prepared to slay his son but who through divine intervention kills a sheep instead. In his poem 'The Parable of the Young Man and the Old' Wilfred Owen alters the story so that the son is slain, along with 'half the seed of Europe, one by one'. Reworking the story again in the Melanesian context, Barker shows us that sometimes at the conjunction of one culture and another a larger truth is revealed.

SAYING THE UNSPEAKABLE

One of the primary issues with which Barker concerns herself in the Trilogy is whether the imagination can come to terms with the monstrous enormity of the war and the apocalyptic sense of loss it involved. Enid Bagnold's strange and uncomfortable *Diary without Dates* (1918) provides in its title an apt metaphor for the inability to contain the First World War and its effects within the few years over which combat took place. The 'Diary', written by the woman much better known for the popular bestseller *National Velvet*, contains the war in miniature. Enid nurses those who have 'shuffled home from death, each having known his life rock on its base', in a military hospital. Her days there feel like a dream: 'I am afraid of waking up and finding it commonplace.'[15] Bagnold's text is imbued with the kind of class and race snobbery that Barker writing at the end of the twentieth century exposes and analyses. Bagnold could not see her way past the prejudices of her time. However, what a comparison shows is the pressing sense of how the indescribable horror of war remains compelling for those who live beyond it. Barker realized on completing *Regeneration* that she had so much more to say and in *The Ghost Road* she has Prior assay that, if the war were to last a hundred years, there might be found a language to say it in.

Rivers suggests the importance of economizing on grief: for Barker the symbolic economy of the text means that no exchange is wasted. Metaphors and epithets resound with particularized meaning in her context, as when Sassoon and Rivers discuss Robert Ross's pacifism:

'I suppose he's learnt to keep his head above the parapet?'
'And you haven't?'
'I don't like holes in the ground.' (R. 54)

Poetry's traditional pursuit of the language of truth and beauty is strained by war. Sensibilities are strained, as when Owen's and Sassoon's conversation oscillates between tense exchanges on the experience of war to talking about the nature of writing. Sassoon comments that the war 'does not lend itself to epics' and Owen sees poetry as something 'to take refuge in', which Barker lets us know in a narratorial aside is 'a point of view he was abandoning even as he spoke' (R. 84). Barker does not move too far away from the general literary consensus that Sassoon's influence on the younger man led Owen to forgo poetic idealism and to forge a gritty poetics of war. Nor does she counter the general estimation of Owen as a 'saintly figure, the victim, the scapegoat' that many from Seamus Heaney to Niall Ferguson have expressed.[16] But she allows her fictional Owen to arrive at many of his own conclusions too and his feelings are supported across the Trilogy: Rivers wants the men in his care to '*feel* the pity and terror' of their war experience in order to begin to combat their fears (R. 48).

Barker emphasizes that language cannot make immediate sense of the war; neither religious discourse nor heroic anthem says the unspeakable. In *The Eye in the Door* Manning, watching the controversial première of Maud Allen as Oscar Wilde's *Salome*, finds he can no longer identify with the sense of passion Wilde conveys, 'the language was impossible for him. France had made it impossible' (ED 78). The reality of war overwhelms the imagination: 'Armageddon, Golgotha, there were no words, a place of desolation so complete no imagination could have invented it' (R. 44). In the 'Declaration' Sassoon rounds on 'the callous complacence with which the majority at home regard the continuation of agonies which they do not share, and which they have not sufficient imagination to realize' (R. 35). Barker enters into an exploration of such unspeakable agonies, as a form of acknowledgement of Sassoon's truth: most of 'The Rest' may well be unable even to come near the truths that the fighting forces share.

The military discourse in which men returning to the Front are 'heroes' and those who remain shell-shocked or traumatized in other ways are 'cases' forces what is irrational and chaotic about the effects of war into a rationalizing lexicon. Across time and with deliberate distance, Barker delves into the agonies of neurasthenia, of military heroism, emotional repression, betrayal and alienation, and imagines the First World War for succeeding generations as a protopathic state of regeneration. Medical and scientific language fails to emote for Sassoon but is reworked to effect by Barker. She also recognizes that the problem of comprehending the enormous tragedy of war is compounded by post-war remembrance and progressively more scientific warfare down the century. Jay Winter, for example, has talked of our general need for what he calls a 'language of mourning', a language of the emotions that can adequately express mourning practices.[17] Barker agrees that 'the search for such a language has been renewed in each generation as if grief is somehow part of the fabric of our consciousness' (AI). Barker purposefully intercuts contemporary parlance with language men would have used in the First World War. She draws the reader's attention to words with very contemporary resonance like 'sexy' (Prior's description of the passion of battle), to ensure that the reader never loses sight of the fact that the meaning of the First World War persists and changes for each generation. In Regeneration, 'Language ran out on you, in the end, the names were left to say it all: Mons, Loos, Ypres, the Somme, Arras' (R. 90). But these names continue to coexist with other markers of war – from each of the wars that have followed.

RIVERS AND PRIOR

W. H. R. Rivers is a transitional figure: his life and work encompass pre-First World War and post-war ideology as he moves through late Victorian to modern times. This enigmatic figure fascinates Barker, who follows the shape of his career through his development from a social anthropologist to a military psychiatrist. Barker captures a historical individual with a few bold strokes. Since Rivers left no diaries or memoirs, dying quite suddenly in 1922, and was, as Blake Morrison has pointed out, 'only a footnote in the history of the Great War',[18] Barker is relatively free to intervene creatively, deriving her sources from his professional writing in *The Todas* (1906), *Instinct and the Unconscious* (1920), and *Conflict and Dream* (1923), and from Sassoon in his memoirs and poems, together with the work of Rivers's biographer Richard Slobodin.[19] In Sassoon's 'Letter to Robert Graves' (1918), Rivers is 'my reasoning Rivers', a father-like figure 'with peace in the pools of his spectacled eyes and a wisely omnipotent grin' whom he begs to 'take' him, and 'make' him, return to the war. Little has changed when he writes about him in 1967. In Rivers's own *Conflict and Dream*, Sassoon also appears as 'Patient B', but the Rivers that persists in Sassoon's memories gathers heroic momentum in the Trilogy.[20]

The consequences of including a historical figure in a fiction can sometimes be the limitation of the fiction. It is a mistake simply to correlate the facts we glean about Rivers with the fiction in the way some critics reduce the work to fit the facts.[21] Tracing Barker's historical framework source by source provides a sense of how meticulous she is in including observations from published records but delimits the extent to which the novels turn on the imagination. At its best, recourse to history ties the balloon of speculation back down to earth and fiction enriches our understanding of the historical. Barker's Rivers is limned out with the same creative energy that she devotes to Billy Prior, but into her characterization of Rivers she incorporates a number of the family legends to which Slobodin refers: he is named after Will Rivers, who shot the man who shot Lord Nelson; he remembers the visits made by Charles Dodgson (aka Lewis Carroll) while writing *Alice in Wonderland*. Most importantly, Rivers is an invention as much as a reclamation: new characteristics enter the frame, like the homoerotic charge that underlies his exchanges with Sassoon. Most reviewers have noted the homosexual feelings that characterize Sassoon's relationships with others, like Graves and Owen, and refer to his citing of Edward Carpenter's *The Intermediate Sex* (1908) as significant. In addition though, Rivers teases out what he calls 'intimate details' (R. 70), and the emotional bond between the two men forms part of Rivers's 'excavating of the ground he stood on' (R. 48). It is Prior who probes this facet of Rivers most effectively, but Rivers's feelings for Sassoon carry the strongest emotional undercurrent.

Barker's Rivers is also something of a messianic figure. With hindsight, the fact that his professional work proved controversial and his intellectual interests influenced significant figures (including T. S. Eliot and Robert Graves, whose theory of poetics derived from Rivers), affords her a rich intellectual context on which to draw. Rivers was certainly not a public performer like Jean-Martin Charcot nor was he an arch theoretician like Freud, but neither has he been pathologized by biographers and critics. Whilst Lacanian psychoanalytical theory continues to presage our contemporary 'Freudian' understanding of psychiatry, Rivers as imagined by Barker (and Slobodin) stands out as a largely independent thinker. His skill in Craiglockhart incorporates the fact that, as a Freudian, rather than dogmatically returning to the men's childhood for the seat of their trauma, or probing their sexuality, he recognizes their disgust at war as the most powerful hinge to the minds he tries to open.[22]

From Rivers and his neurological work with Henry Head, Barker derives a scientific model that she reworks as a literary trope. The suturing of broken nerves the two undertook as an experiment long before the onset of war is traced as the process of regeneration. It involves two distinct stages: the first is 'sensation', pain that is difficult to quantify or to localize (the 'protopathic'); the second is a form of control whereby the subject begins gradually to locate the pain and to control his reaction to it (the 'epicritic'). The two terms invented by Rivers and Head form part of a larger dialectic: the epicritic is frenzied and anarchic while the protopathic is rational – or rationalizing. Barker deconstructs this apparently tight and classical binary opposition through Rivers, who is torn between his professional function – to restore the men in his care from protopathic hell to the more restrained level at which they can conduct themselves in 'manly' fashion in war – and his deep-seated fear that he cannot heal them. Rivers, like his men, is vulnerable, split. Like Prior while working in Intelligence in *The Eye in the Door*, Rivers is part of the war machine that gathers up those men who have wandered from the established ground on which the war can be fought, and sets them back on a socially sanctioned path back to the trenches.

Rivers's consultations with Prior begin as confrontations, and this feature of their relationship, as instigated by Prior, is never fully allayed. Exchanges are almost universally tense and emotionally discordant (*ED* 132–40) and for Rivers their sessions become exhausting. Rivers believes their conflictual behaviour has a strong father–son element, but this is a safety net. Barker makes clear that it does not supersede other descriptors. Prior, in many ways, has stalked Rivers across their numerous therapy sessions, and, shortly before returning to the Front for the final time, while describing a dream, he lets slip his love for the older man: 'the faces on the revolver targets . . . turned into the faces of people I love. But only after I'd pulled the trigger so there was nothing I could do about it. 'Fraid I killed you every time' (*GR* 98). The homoerotic charge that suffuses many of Prior's exchanges across the novels is diffused by father–son tension here but present nevertheless, as it is in Rivers's gentle treatment of Sassoon, a man with whom he feels more at ease. Where the warmth that Rivers and Sassoon feel in each other's presence is comfortably mutual, Prior taunts Rivers in ungentlemanly fashion while trying to probe his feelings. He even goes so far as to 'diagnose' Rivers in the most basic and direct terms, bending psychoanalysis to take a pop at his mentor. Barker has said on a number of occasions that Prior was originally created 'purely to get up Rivers's nose: every characteristic of Prior is something that the historical Rivers would have found difficult; the working-class background, his bisexuality and the fact that he perceives sexual ambivalence in Rivers' (AI).

Prior may clash with Rivers, but surprisingly they also have certain things in common. Rivers has lost his visual memory, a loss he has traced back to a repressed incident at the age of 5, after which he 'put his mind's eye out'. Prior, on the other hand, is beset by a specific visual memory that haunts him waking or sleeping, Tower's eyeball. Like so many of the officers he treats at Craiglockhart, Rivers is afflicted with a 'paralytic' stammer, which he basically controls in adulthood, but it is uncomfortably close to the neurotic stammers and twitches that afflict the shell-shocked victims to whom he administers help. Prior notices what Rivers can usually hide and, like Prior, Rivers has not fully faced his demons. It remains unclear precisely what events in Rivers's childhood have been pushed down into his subconscious. In bringing Prior into Rivers's orbit, Barker strengthens our understanding of the tension between masculine resilience and vulnerability. In these two characters she locates the most potent themes of the Trilogy.

SEX AND DEATH

Barker is the first writer of fiction to pursue in depth the visceral excitement of war. Recently, as Barker herself has noted, it has become almost taboo to discuss the physical attractions of war for young men in ways that foreground not just heroism but the passion of battle. Barker does not flinch from exposing the sexual frisson that Prior describes when going 'over the top'. In *Mrs Dalloway* Woolf's Septimus Smith describes the war as a 'little shindy' of 'schoolboys with gunpowder', conveying an ironic and bitter sense of ghoulish excitement. But Barker can go much further, exposing war as an aphrodisiac, drawing on Rivers's memories of the headhunters in Melanesia, where headhunting provided the 'life' of the community. The sexual excitement that Prior describes when engaged in battle is as fascinating as it is repelling. He describes it as 'sexy': 'racing blood, risk, physical exposure, a kind of awful *daring* about it' (*GR* 172). Claire M. Tylee in her survey of women's writing on war states that killing usually 'acts like a shutter on women's imagination' so that murder in war becomes 'part of the forbidden zone on which they do not trespass'. Barker has extrapolated on a facet of the war experience that has eluded or perhaps frightened other writers but that was first examined by some of the soldiers themselves.[23] She notes that, in one of Wilfred Owen's letters, 'he talks about "exposing himself openly", and it is a very strange figure of speech to be using for that experience. It juxtaposes sex and death in a way that interests me' (AI). She explains that it was her intention to make this idea more explicit through Prior. Owen's letters are a primary source. Written to his mother, Susan Owen, they contain unusually graphic references to battle, death, and despair.[24] Sex and death are yoked together in disturbing ways in the Trilogy, largely through Billy Prior, but in *Border Crossing* Barker returns to this difficult topic. Tom Seymour dives into the dangerous waters to rescue a young man from what he believes to be a suicide attempt. Afterwards he is emotionally taut ('he was staring at his own death') and the sex he has with his wife has little to do with love or with their avowed attempts to conceive a child. Tom uses sex to feel his way back to life. However, later, they lie in bed 'side by side, a medieval knight and lady on a tomb' (*BC* 11), the funereal image yoking together sex and death to give the lie to their love: their marriage is dying.

In the Trilogy, Prior proves a reliable judge of sexual character for the reader. He sees through the vagaries of priests like the Reverend Arthur Lindsey, whom Sarah's mother seeks to impress, and Ada Lumb herself (*GR* 68–71), whom Barker describes as a 'malevolent force', setting herself against her daughter's love affair while indulging herself by reading salacious stories (AI). In fact, one of the key ways in which sex and death are conjoined is in the form of Barker's gallows humour. Reading the *Hydra* and most particularly Owen's contributions, Barker noted a 'terrible, facetious, mocking medieval humour' (AI). Major Telford in *The Ghost Road* believes a nurse has cut off his 'penis' but that he can still urinate with his 'cock'. Moffet's failed suicide attempt ends with him entertaining others with bizarre stories of his horse developing gangrene (*GR* 59). Time and again, Barker entangles the most difficult of emotions in a dry and knowing laugh, reminding us of the incredibly physical rush of life that follows the fear of death. Across the Trilogy, Barker demystifies sex in all its forms, just as she did in *Blow Your House Down*. In *The Eye in the Door*, Lizzie McDowell (Mac's mother) commits the 'patriotic gesture' of having sex with all seven of the local men who sign up to fight – including Mac's schoolboy friend Billy Prior. Prior's sexuality and his sexual encounters are as much a feature of war as its backdrop. His hatred of prostitution is a reaction to the abuse he suffered from Father MacKenzie as a child and charging money to the priest for sex is an angry child's rebuttal.

Prior's final sexual encounter with a young French boy in *The Ghost Road* is pure farce. Barker punctures any pretence of near-death passion with Prior's sardonically sick memory of the European anthem, 'O, ye millions I embrace you, This kiss is for the whole world . . .', as his sperm meets that of the many Germans who have had sex with the young French boy while 'passing through' the village. The boy becomes the 'seminal spittoon' that Prior described as his own role when first having sex with Charles Manning in *The Eye in the Door*. Barker has alerted us to the ways that sex across the Trilogy operates as 'a movement downwards, from beginning to end, towards a more brutal encounter' (AI). In this final sex act in war, with a 16-year-old boy in exchange for cigarettes, Prior hits 'bottom'; nuzzling the boy's 'tight French sphincter', he is left neurotically hoping he will not contract a sexual disease when within pages a single bullet will put paid to the character whose vibrancy, and wry flouting of authority, have coloured the pages of three novels

VISUALIZING THE TRILOGY

The Trilogy is often very visually effective. Barker succeeds in creating powerful anti-war images of waste and chaos in the trenches, reminiscent of Frank Wright's graphic and cinematic descriptions in *Liza's England*. Barker allows that her emphasis on dialogue and the unfolding of story through the nuancing of repeated imagery could be considered 'filmic'.[25] Among the most visually evocative images are the mystical scenes set in France in *The Ghost Road*. They seem more reminiscent of Alain-Fournier's classic *Le Grand Meaulnes* (1912) – translated into English as *The Lost Domain* – than British writing out of the war, except perhaps for Robert Graves's short poem 'The Morning before Battle'.[26] Prior, Owen, and fellow officers Polts and Hallett are granted temporary respite in a deserted house in France close to Amiens. The house is a ghostly ruin in a French village where there are 'extraordinary jagged shapes of broken walls in moonlight, silver mountains and chasms, with here and there black pits of craters thronged in weeds' (*GR* 179). In the midst of the war, seemingly forgotten for a moment, the men find themselves in a house half-reclaimed by Nature. They create a 'fragile civilization' and Barker draws back as the reader watches the men drink wine, pick roses, and long to be left there out of harm's way in their 'fellowship on the brink of disaster' (*GR* 143). The house the men share is baroque and seems enchanted. They prepare their new environment theatrically, moving furniture from other derelict properties and creating visual set pieces like 'still life'. But the ethereal house is broken and it bleeds 'quietly from its unstaunchable wound' (*GR* 145). The soldiers are stopped in time but keenly aware that this hiatus is the calm before the final storm in which their lives will be stopped short. If this quiet sequence is emotionally disturbing, Barker has noted how culturally resonant was the final episode of the cult TV comedy *Blackadder* in this regard. In the final episode of the series devoted to the First World War, the viewer follows Captain Blackadder and his men 'over the top', from slow motion into the freeze-frame in which they are frozen in death, until a dissolve vitiates into the blood-red poppies of Armistice.

Where *Blackadder* catches tragedy up in comedy, Gillies MacKinnon's film adaptation of *Regeneration* (1997) reinforces the tragic waste of war in visually literate terms. A Scottish–Canadian co-production, *Regeneration* was released in the same year as the Hollywood blockbuster *Saving Private Ryan* and *The Thin Red Line*. Despite its critical acclaim, and the fact that it is by far the more articulate film, it has been overshadowed by journalists who spend much more time on the other war films of that year. Nevertheless, *Regeneration* received glowing reviews and academy award nominations.[27] MacKinnon, through Allan Scott's screenplay, remains close to the novel but is not constrained by it.[28] Clearly, the film cannot render all the complexities of the literature: it is a different kind of text functioning in a different medium and through a different language. In the film, visual images of young disabled men, sharing space at Craiglockhart with neurasthenic officers, bring home the physicality of war to show how the fighting cauterized young lives. Such scenes are not present in the novel. The hypnagogic hallucinations Barker has Sassoon suffer, and which help him decide to return to active duty, are also visually effective in the sequence where puzzled dead men from his platoon circle his bed in the way he describes in the poems 'Sick Leave' and 'Banishment', both written at Craiglockhart. Importantly, as Barker wrote into her subject, she says the idea of place *as* character became more coherent. Barker says she became very aware when writing *Regeneration* of Craiglockhart itself. Whereas Union Street is not delineated because it functions metaphorically and the Palmerston in *Blow Your House Down* works similarly, the men's rooms in Craig-lockhart Hospital are dugouts in the dark. The film imparts the deep, ruddy red texture of the corridors of Craiglockhart. The fields around the hospital where Prior and Sarah make love are suffused with browns and reds and the battlefields are sepia-sodden, from the ubiquitous men's uniforms to the colour of their bloody dreams.

One is reminded of Sir Henry Newbolt's poem 'The War Films', which relates specifically to footage of the Battle of the Somme. Its opening line, 'O living pictures of the dead', is an apparently oxymoronic contradiction in terms, dramatized by the skulls embedded in mud that comprise MacKinnon's opening panoramic shots. Skulls are a key motif across the Trilogy and in this way something of the novel's symbolic resonance is captured, primarily through Owen's idea of skulls growing like mushrooms out of the mud (*R.* 84). Glen Macpherson's cinematography – the trenches, bomb craters, corpses, and human remains – is a reminder that on the first day of the Battle of the Somme, for example, the British lost some 60,000 men in full-frontal attacks against the German Second Army and that by the end one and a quarter million men had lost their lives. The camera pans across the dead and dying in No Man's Land as bombs whistle and light up the killing zone. The film cuts to the Edinburgh countryside around Craiglockhart where small animals are strung up in a tree and a naked man sits amidst their detritus. Two bleak scenes coalesce to evoke the horror of a war that cannot be confined to the battlefields. A few frames later Sassoon's statement that the war has been deliberately prolonged leads Rivers to declare that he is suffering from 'a very powerful anti-war neurosis' despite his Military Cross. The film success-fully distils key aspects of the novel and builds on others. It succeeds in evoking Sassoon's struggle with honesty against capitulation, and it conveys something of the horror and pity of war, including disturbing scenes of soldiers shocked with electricity to 'cure' them of war neuroses.

Where the film falls down is in its refusal to pursue the homoeroticism that charges exchanges between men in Barker's fiction. Rather the film turns on symbiotic literary friendships (Graves and Sassoon and Owen and Sassoon) In the film Owen's role is more pronounced than in the novel, as if to counter W. B. Yeats's infamous dismissal of First World War poets by omitting them from the *Oxford Book of Modern Verse* (1936), asserting that the war poet 'felt bound to plead the suffering of his men' when 'passive suffering is not a theme for poetry'.[29] Yeats clearly had Owen in mind, since shortly before his death he had been collecting his poetry and drafting a preface in which he famously stated that his subject was the pity of war. Certainly the film 'streamlines Barker's complex novel considerably' as Westman has argued,[30] by emphasizing the literary and cross-generational relationship over the ho-moerotic. But it successfully translates the horror of war to the screen and something of the tenderness between the men.

At the end of the Trilogy, Billy Prior expounds a theory as to why soldiers write letters, poems, and diaries as 'a way of claiming community': 'First-person narrators can't die, so long as we keep telling the story of our own lives we're safe. Ha fucking Ha' (*GR* 115). Importantly, Barker resists the very strategy that she has Prior undermine here: the autobiographi-cal. To tell her stories in the first-person confessional mode might have proved more immediately emotive, creating a character as the origin of all meaning. But it also presupposes that it is possible to create a single and intelligible subject position within the contradictory discourses of war. Ford Madox Ford's Christopher Tietjens in *Parade's End* (1924–8) tries to tidy his thoughts of war – through first-person narration – but they threaten to break him apart. Barker's 'I' dissolves into pieces in *The Eye in the Door* when Prior feels at his most exposed; Rivers 'puts his own eye [or "I"] out' when he represses his visual memory in childhood and he worries that a single story of war would diminish the power of multiple and changing stories. Barker's predominant narrational model reflects the same tension between involvement and distance that the reader prizes in Rivers. In *Regeneration*, Sassoon describes Rivers's treatment of war neuroses as requiring an 'exercise of sympathy and detachment combined'. It is this stress-provoking daily negotiation for Rivers that provides an analogy for Barker's literary aesthetic. The analogy – monitored by a controlling presence sensitive to the situations of those who do not easily fit into the system – augments the patina of memory that characterizes the *Trilogy* and much of Barker's writing.

6

Looking Forward into the Past: *Another World*

> The rank stench of those bodies haunts me still,
> And I remember things I'd best forget.
>
> (Siegfried Sassoon, 'A Night Attack', 1916)

RUMINATIONS ON WAR

Suzie MacKenzie, after interviewing Barker in 1998, asserted that there was 'nothing predictive' in her novels: 'you will learn nothing about the future ... in this sense she is supremely ahistorical.'[1] But *Another World* takes its epigraph from Joseph Brodsky, 'Remember: the past won't fit into memory without something left over; it must have a future.' It is shot through with disquieting reminders of the ways in which memory is reconfigured in the present and for the future. In fact, the entire novel is written in the present continuous – the eternal present in which we live out our lives. The use of the present tense creates a disturbing effect, especially when we remember that the present is itself historic in that the past figures largely in our understanding of it – so largely that, for Geordie Lucas, 101-year-old veteran of the First World War, the past has overtaken his present: 'it's not like remembering it, it's like he's actually seeing it' (*AW* 69). Geordie's past has become a physical burden he carries into the future.

Past war and present guilt are made analogous with purgatory at the end of a century in which religion suffered a period of declension and new age spirituality or alternative

80

philosophies provide no sanctuary for a dying man. In the final pages of the novel, Nick suddenly realizes that his grandfather's dying words, 'I am in hell', were stuck in the present tense, a 'recognized symptom of post-traumatic stress disorder', a term Geordie may not have known but can be made to fit. As contemporary psychologists create neologisms to preserve for the future their definitions of human trauma, Barker shows that not all their ideas are new. One is reminded by the simplicity of Geordie's final words that they represent the death of the Christ-like figure in Wilfred Owen's 'Strange Meeting': 'By his dead smile I knew we stood in Hell.' They also echo Sassoon's 'I died in hell – (They call it Passchendaele)' in the poem 'Memorial Tablet'. Geordie's death may have been deferred, but Barker weaves a story in which the most memorable character is a man who has a scornful scepticism for the safety of the narrative past. Geordie is arrested in time. Unlike Liza Wright, who seems to float across the years catching a thought here and a meaning there, Geordie is caught in a moment that is relentlessly repeated for him.

Critics often question the security of the past tense for writers of fiction. For Roland Barthes it is 'an image of an order ... one of those numerous formal pacts between the writer and society for the justification of the former and the serenity of the latter'.[2] There is little serenity in *Another World*, for Geordie or for his descendants. As the novel closes, Nick remembers the trip he took with his grandfather to the French battlefields to visit the 'ageless graves for those who were never permitted to grow old' (*AW* 278). It echoes a trip Barker herself took as televised in *On the Ghost Road* and it stands as a reminder that the First World War has never exhausted itself as a subject for public debate or for fiction. As Prior notes in *The Ghost Road*, 'Fifty years from now a farmer'll be ploughing these fields and turn up skulls' (*GR* 240) and the grave sites Barker visited in France were bathed in controversy in 2000 when their maintenance seemed to be in jeopardy.[3] Nick is repelled by the arches at Thiepval, while for Geordie they seem to effect a symbolic exchange by which to graft his memories on to his grandson. Geordie's story does not exist in a social vacuum.

Another World chronicles the last days of 101-year-old Geordie Lucas, whose mind turns on events in the First World

War, so that he believes he is dying from a bayonet wound he sustained in the run-up to the Somme in 1916, rather than the cancer that has finally defeated his fighting spirit at the end of the twentieth century. The novel is riven with ironies that pit the present against the past. Of the thirty-nine million corpses we know the war left behind, the bayonet wound was an unusual injury to sustain. The war may have commenced with infantry and bayonets, but at its close horses had been superseded by tanks, and bayonets by bombs. Geordie is at one and the same time unusual and representative – in his advanced age he may be unusual but he stands for a lost generation and, whether or not he chooses the responsibility, he is judged to speak for his comrades-in-arms. This is precisely how he comes to be viewed by those who wait for him to die: his elderly daughter, his grandson (a university lecturer in psychology), and his interviewer (a writer and historian). Geordie's nightmares of battle return with a vengeance after decades of relatively undisturbed sleep. One episode in particular draws out the power of memory. Staying overnight with his grandfather, Nick is awakened when the old man sleepwalks out into the cold, and begins inching his way across the cobbles as if crawling through the trenches. Geordie is living in a mental world of the war's making and Nick must grapple for words that will cross the time that separates the men. Finally he says, 'We've got to get back. It's nearly light' (*AW* 162) and lulls the weeping veteran back into the house. Nick cannot protect Geordie from the past that overwhelms him like a living nightmare, nor when his grandfather comes to, disoriented and uncomprehending, can Nick console him that the experience is truly or finally past.

In the last months of the centenarian's life, he clings to his guilt over the death of his brother Harry during the war. The wound he received then is the thing to which he can cleave most firmly – a physical trace of his emotional scarring. Whereas under hypnosis Billy Prior re-enacts the past in *Regeneration*, Geordie invests his memories with the guilt that floods his present. Wounds remain as scars, but they continue to leak, stretch, and weep; they embody the war. For Geordie, remembering the past is visceral, like 'falling through a trapdoor into another room, and it's still going on' (*AW* 265).

For Geordie, Harry's body remains in No Man's Land in 1916, but he continues to be present in nightmares in which Geordie finds himself falling into Harry's screaming mouth. When Geordie says 'I killed Harry' (*AW* 164), Nick immediately reads the declaration as metaphor, but discovers after the old man's death that he had to stop his wounded brother from screaming and bringing the German army down on the rest of the battalion. He crawled out alone into No Man's Land and silenced him with a quick death. In Geordie feelings of survivor's guilt and unacknowledged grief and anger come together. Barker explores the tangle of emotions in a multi-layered narrative in which Robert Fanshawe, son of a Victorian entrepreneur, also kills his brother. In 1904, the boy kills a younger sibling but, acquitted, goes on to fight in Geordie's war; his guilt attaches itself to the same conflict. Before he dies, Robert reminds his conspirator sister to 'remember how young we were' (*AW* 113), a tired signal of forgiveness that precedes his own death in war. In *Another World*, Barker expatiates on two axiomatic phrases, 'during the war . . .' and 'getting away with murder', in a way that makes clear what Gilles Deleuze has described in another context: 'The body is never in the present, it contains the before and after, tiredness and waiting. Tiredness and waiting, even despair are the attitudes of the body.'[4]

FRAMING WAR EXPERIENCE

Critics like Elaine Scarry in *The Body in Pain* (1985) and Marita Sturken in *Tangled Memories* (1997) have described how those wounded in war function as vehicles for memorialization so that the veteran becomes a war memorial in himself. The veteran's body and the state are often conflated in symbolic rhetoric. He is a vehicle for a society coming to terms with the effects of war – even for national healing. In Barker's novel, Geordie is an interlocutor; he speaks for the war generation to those generations that follow, specifically the children in the primary schools Barker has him visit. Helen, a colleague of Nick's but in the History department of his university, has written a book on veterans' memories of combat as altered by changing public perceptions of war and commemoration.

Geordie is one of her primary sources and their interview is a published part of her book entitled *Soldier, from the Wars Returning*. But, unlike Helen, who can move on to the next project, Geordie is unable to find an ending to the war narrative inscribed on his body, except in death. Sturken asks, 'Does healing mean a foreclosing or an expansion of the discourse of war?'[5] It is a question Barker too exposes and explores through guilt and atonement, memory and amnesia, across the Trilogy and, with contemporary resonance, in this more recent novel, in which the effects of war are a reminder of evils in the past and a warning of adversity in the future. Barker provides the reader with a series of ways in which to read Geordie, his memories, and the people with whom he has relationships.

Helen introduces Geordie's public voice, but Nick's training in psychology leads him to refute the idea of public memory and to assert that memory is 'a biochemical change in an individual brain, and that's all there is' (*AW* 85). However, Nick is led by his feelings for his grandfather over and above the methodologies he has learned. Only after Geordie's death does he slip into academic formulations, as in the use of the term 'post-traumatic stress disorder', touched on above. As academics reach for metaphors and models, they risk losing sight of the individual behind the terminology. For example, Geordie remains a passionate man; old age has diminished neither romance nor libido. His longing for his wife, dead so many years before, is achingly present in a song he sings in remembrance of her during an interview with Helen; romance flickers as he flirts with Helen and gradually develops into genuine feeling; and he is reported to have had an intensely sexual relationship aged 78 with a bri-nylon leopard-skin-clad widow with an 'opulent bosom'. This last relationship is reminiscent of Stephen's elderly Aunt Clem and her sexual relationship with 'fancy man' Joe in *Liza's England*. Nick, like Stephen in the earlier novel, is disturbed by the sexuality of the elderly and even flinches at the sight of Geordie's genitals forming part of what he sees as a 'frail and dauntless body' (*AW* 127). Barker's elderly characters do not conform to easy stereotypes and those younger characters that underestimate them are usually forced to re-examine the stereotypical patterns into which their assumptions have atrophied.

Geordie does not conform to the general public's changing views about war. Post-traumatic stress disorder, the terminology his grandson uses, and the interviews that Helen conducts with Geordie produce a fruitful tension between theorizing about memory – and agonizing over its tenacity. Helen believes veterans remember communal myths rather than personal experience, that their stories may be collective and even apocryphal. Helen's intention is to persuade Geordie to 'frame his war experiences in terms of late twentieth-century preoccupations. Gender. Definitions of masculinity. Homoeroticism' (*AW* 83). But, as W. H. R. Rivers became aware, analytic method will not always dictate response and Geordie will not be made over by the changing views the historian detects. His recollections are personal even if they have a collective resonance and they are resistant to change and to fashion. Barker ensures they are also redolent of vernacular rather than 'official' cultural expression: 'one time there was six of us by the side of the road and I'd ate something that didn't agree with me. I just had to do a runner fast as I could. I was squatting down with me trousers round me ankles when a shell come over and they'd gone. You see you can't make sense of that, can you? I got the squitters, so I'm alive. Where's the sense in that?' (*AW* 149).

Geordie represents what it *feels* like to carry the guilt of wartime atrocities not what it should be like to recall them more cogently as time passes. One is reminded of Stephen's father, Walter, in *Liza's England* when he bemoans, 'You talk about *passing* time, *killing* time, and you don't know what you're on about. You don't kill time, time kills you' (*LE* 117). In the same novel, Frank evinces feelings about the grimy, suffocating realities of combat casualties long after the battle has passed. His First World War experience is the most intense and meaningful distillation of his life. Even a child's game, playing toy soldiers with his son, transports Frank back in a singular rush to the trenches. Each of his senses takes him back to 'another world':

Soon the crackling of the fire was a village burning . . .
A shell burst, sending showers of earth and stones into the air. Billy was down. Frank ran to help, only to find his hand caught and held.

'You can't do that, Dad. He's *dead*.'
Frank stared. 'Oh yes. Yes,' he said, 'I'd forgotten that.'
His fist was clenched. Slowly he lowered it and forced the fingers
to uncurl. (*LE* 96–7)

In earlier work Barker allows the narrator access to the
interior world of former soldiers like Frank. Such sequences
detail the swirling of thoughts and fears and the hot panic of
memory. In more recent fiction she has stripped away the layers
of prose, replacing them with dialogue. Neither Geordie nor
Danny Miller in *Border Crossing* may be apprehended as clearly
as Frank Wright. Geordie and Helen and Danny and Tom play
out relationships based in conversation – in therapy – and they
represent a clash of interests, albeit bound up in warm repartee
and a supportive framework as in *Another World*. What Geordie
does not say is important and what the narrator avoids saying
leaves an area of shadow around the work. Pierre Macherey
encourages us to read the shadow as absence or as the partial
presence of something more than surface detail.[6] We read what
is implicit and are reminded of Barker's statement that dialogue
is 'sculpted silence', and silence too a source of expression.

For Freud the absence of words is the 'unconscious' and a
Freudian reading of the novel would confirm that that which
is repressed returns to haunt the individual who hides from its
import: Geordie has not confronted the emotional effects of
war over a long life. He has refused the 'talking cure': Nick
remembers his grandfather as silent when he was young and,
as he grew older, he 'never talked' about the war (*AW* 163).
Rather than dramatize trauma, Barker's psychoanalytical perspective opens out the effects through what Stendhal called the
'petits faits vrais', the novelist's concern with daily life at its
most mundane. These moments are marked most precisely as
systematic repression. Nick remembers his grandfather would
walk a mile out of his way to avoid passing a war memorial.
But he also recalls that Geordie's refusal to talk about the war
was oddly offset by his habit of looking into a scratched and
cracked mirror that he had carried on his person throughout
the war and continued to use for shaving each morning.

In 'The Storyteller' (1936), Walter Benjamin judges that
soldiers returning from the First World War were 'poorer in

communicable experience'. Such incommunicability involves silence and grief. Harry and his death in 1916 is the 'central silence' or 'dark star' in *Another World* (*AW* 158). The sheer inability to make sense of the experience – or the impossibility of telling the experience of war truly – is captured by Benjamin in natural imagery:

> A generation that had gone to school on a horse-drawn streetcar now stood under the open sky in a countryside in which nothing remained unchanged but the clouds, and beneath these clouds, in a field of force of destructive torrents and explosions, was the tiny, fragile human body.[7]

In the Trilogy, Barker turns to the soldiers' bodies and to their minds. In *Another World* her emphasis on memory and how it succeeds and fails in mastering the self and the body takes the reader back to Frank in *Liza's England*. However, without the comfort of religious belief to console or faith in the kinds of myth and ritual that energize the seances over which Frank presides, Barker forces readers to examine loss in contemporary terms: without community or faith. Religion is a subject that 'never came up' in Nick's talks with his grandfather and he can answer none of the vicar's questions as to the old man's beliefs. At the funeral he wonders whether Geordie believed in a redeemer at all.

A MILLENNIAL FAMILY ROMANCE

Geordie is not alone in his loss of faith. In many different ways, the novel explores the legacy of the *Regeneration Trilogy* in its millenarian concerns for Geordie's descendants and his extended family, immersed in a tangle of contemporary problems. Young Gareth plays at war, glued to his computer screen, to video games like *Streetfighter* and to films like *Terminator 2*. The macabre, sensual enthusiasm that Prior feels in 'going over the top' is changed by the end of the century into a gruesome fascination with the simulacrum of warfare, while Nick, late to collect his 13-year-old daughter from Newcastle railway station, tortures himself with potent media images of violence and abuse:

A few months ago, a fourteen-year-old girl was thrown from a train by some yob who hadn't got anywhere when he tried to chat her up ... Peter Sutcliffe's bearded face, the number plate of a house on Cromwell Street, three figures smudged on a video surveillance screen, an older boy taking a toddler by the hand while his companion strides ahead, eager for the atrocity to come. (*AW* 3)

Fear and apprehension are never far below the quotidian round of this university lecturer's musings and in this sense the novel represents an important stage in Barker's exploration of contemporary social anxieties. Geordie, Nick, and Gareth represent three different ways of engaging with violence across three generations. Linda Grant notes how the generations 'squirm uncomfortably' when confronted with alternative viewpoints on – or impulses towards – violence:

Those who lived through it, don't talk about it and are only now beginning to engage publicly (and perhaps even privately) with the trauma of half a century ago [veterans of the Second World War and by extension the minority of veterans like Geordie from the First]; those who have never known it and want to engineer it socially out of existence [Nick]; and those who have never known it but flirt with it in a new way [Gareth] ...[8]

The family is a site of contested meaning. In his study of the 'family romance' Sigmund Freud argued that 'the whole purpose of society rests on the opposition between successive generations'.[9] Nick replaces his own father with his grandfather Geordie, who better fulfils the role. Frieda behaves as much like Geordie's wife as his daughter. Gareth's family romance is the stuff of sci-fi, as in *Terminator 2*, where 'terminators' are sent into 1995 to protect 10-year-old John Connor or to kill him. Roles are not always fixed, but inter-generational conflict in *Another World* is largely unacknowledged and unspoken. If marriage constitutes the bedrock of the family, Nick and Fran, embarking on their second, find there is tension between their first and second families, especially between Nick and Gareth, the stepson who spends forty hours a week playing computer games and thinks Nick a 'lousy' stepfather.

Christine Bridgewood has noted that the family saga is markedly different from other genres of popular fiction (notably the romance) in its 'lack of drive towards narrative closure and in its tendency to begin at the point where romance stops'.[10] Barker is careful to emphasize the ways in which the family in this novel is sited precariously – emotionally and psychologically if not materially. She allows that she had hoped that the domestic setting of *Another World* might provide relief from the gloom of Craiglockhart and the trenches (AI). Contradictorily, the claustrophobia of Lob's Hill and the unrelieved tensions within the family unsettle in very specific ways. Continual reiteration that 'we are a family' exacerbates the yawning chasm between the ideal of family and the characters' fractured reality. For Gareth, family togetherness is 'crap' and he fails to see the point of the family unit. He distances himself from the others at the first opportunity – when out shopping with his mother, at the beach with the family, and even when simply at home, retreating to his room and spending hours alone there. In fact, as soon as the novel opens Barker cuts between Nick, caught off guard by his daughter's lack of physical affection for him and her barely understood jokes about sex, and Fran back home. Fran recoils at the thought of her own son's hand on her shoulder; guilt as to whether she has been a 'good' mother has sabotaged her capacity for easy affection.

The foundation of the family is the home, and, in one of the only scenes in which Nick, Fran, Gareth, and Miranda are coordinated, they work together to reveal a Victorian family on whom their own lives are palimpsested. Removing the original wallpaper from their living room walls, the late-twentieth-century family sees itself reflected in the strained and disconcerting faces of the Fanshawes. What they reveal is 'an exercise in hate' (*AW* 40). They stand before a grotesque and ghostly parody of themselves as Victorian paterfamilias. The symbolism is starker than one usually finds in Barker's work. In fact, Miranda states, 'It's us' and Nick discovers later that Lob's Hill was the site of a murder within the Victorian family. The symbolism is finally undercut by Nick; 'It's easy to let oneself be dazzled by false analogies – the past never threatens anything as simple, or as avoidable, as repetition' (*AW* 278). Earlier, in *Liza's England*, Stephen realizes that the flat he occupies in a dilapidated Victorian house is part of the home where Liza's mother performed domestic duties and Liza visited as a child. The Wynyards, like the Fanshawes in *Another World*, owned the munitions factory and functioned as pseudo-aristocracy in a poor community. Whereas such connections are one thread in the community Barker knits together from Liza's memory, in *Another World* they ghost the present in more chilling ways. The Fanshawes seem to be safeguarding the past as heritage industry, through the stately home that families like Nick's now comfortably visit on summer days, while hiding the secret of fratricide, a crime committed and then contained within the family. Visiting Fleet House, the Fanshawe residence after Lob's Hill, Nick discovers the finished copy of the family portrait that unnerved him so on his wall at home, out of public view, hidden in an alcove that has been cordoned off. He discovers the story of the murder of the youngest boy, James, as committed by the older children, Robert and Muriel, in a book by a historical novelist he has even met once or twice. But most disturbing of all, he sees a physical manifestation of guilt and sadness.

Ghosts represent a powerful force of memory for a range of contemporary writers. Here they form part of Nick's hallucination, Miranda's second sight, and Gareth's sense that, even alone in his room, there is another unearthly presence. When Nick, Miranda, and Gareth each see a girl, we are expected to realize that they may each be seeing the same girl, a spectre of the Fanshawe daughter whose guilt for killing her baby brother coalesces as her own physical shape persisting into the present. Barker argues: 'The simple explanation of delusion or mental illness is not a possible explanation. It's the visual equivalent of Geordie's voice on the tape, which is a *real* voice though he is dead. Perhaps the girl at the window is a "real" image although the girl is dead' (AI). One is reminded that Barker cites the influence of Henry James's *The Turn of the Screw* (1898) on this novel and that the pervasive sense of disquiet and imminent evil can be understood to emanate from what the protagonists fear in the present and for the future, rather than what may have happened in the past.

Nevertheless, Nick feels frightened that his children are overshadowed by the evil he discovers at the root of the Fanshawe family. Barker has Miranda compare Lob's Hill, 'one of the few houses left that's still a family home' (*AW* 12), to Brontë's Wuthering Heights and the quick analogy triggers tragic associations. Later, she wishes she had a book like *Jane Eyre* (1847) to relieve the boredom of sitting with family members. Catherine Belsey, in her study of the English novel, points out that young Jane had less understanding of her circumstances than the reader, and in *Wuthering Heights* (1847) neither Lockwood nor Nellie Dean apprehends the true meaning of the relationship between Cathy and Heathcliff.[11] Miranda's depressive mother, absent throughout the novel, has been 'sectioned' in an effort to control her mental illness and there is no mention in the novel of any support her daughter may have been offered. Miranda is simply a girl who is 'unable' to think about what has happened to her mother and Nick's first wife is locked away in an institution in typically nineteenth-century gothic style.

The female characters one would expect to find as protagonists in the popular Victorian family saga (Fran and Barbara, Miranda and Frieda) are carefully removed to the background in *Another World*. Instead, it is Nick who negotiates around much of the anxiety of family life and who takes primary responsibility for Geordie. But Barker demonstrates that the phenomenon of the 'New Man' at the end of the twentieth century was characterized as least as much by continuity as by changes in gender roles. Fran still takes all the responsibility in the home, despite her advancing pregnancy. The reader shares knowledge with the author of the ways in which *Another World* participates in and undermines the family romance, and the ways in which the novel comments on the classic realism and gothic horror of the Victorian novel form. Each allusion to Victoriana – Geordie is, of course, born during her reign and in the Queen Victoria Hospital in Newcastle – reinforces the overlaying of one century with another and one set of novelistic conventions with another. At one point Fran declares, 'It's nobody's fault' (*AW* 92), echoing Arthur Clennam's lament in Dickens's *Little Dorrit* (1857) and reminding us of his emphasis on individual responsibility for social ills. The novel is set in a Newcastle dominated by Anthony Gormley's postmodern 200-tonne steel sculpture, the Angel of the North. Amid the mosaic of allusions that intertwine the nineteenth century with the twentieth in the novel, we are reminded that Fran is no 'Angel of the House', to borrow Coventry Patmore's famous phrase epitomizing the perfect Victorian wife. Fran is bitter and feels like a woman under siege. Even cooking a family meal is an irritating dilemma: the potatoes boil dry and the family force themselves to eat in silence. Fran is heavily pregnant: she lacks sleep and snags her varicose veins in the child safety gate, and Nick is repulsed by her sheer physicality (*AW* 92–3).

Published in 1998, *Another World* responds to right-wing rhetoric about the stability and morality of the family by creating something of an 'anti-family' saga: the new Christian Right's message that the family functions as a means to 'recover' lost meaning as well as a lost past is cleverly undermined when the Victorian past that is revealed crosses family happiness with murder and the same kind of unending guilt from which Geordie is suffering. Thatcherite soundbites on the Victorian family proved an ironic example to choose through which to 'teach' family values in the 1980s. But it was an analogy that operated ideologically to mask those facets of society that were being systematically dismantled. As Michael Neve succinctly puts it, the Victorian family 'generated a literature screaming with misery or loneliness or cruelty', which towards the end of the twentieth century was 'confected as a family romance with all that volume turned off, except for a soundtrack combining muzak and moral niceties in equal measure'.[12] The ideology of domesticity and what Michele Barrett calls the 'moral desirability' of the family developed out of Victorian restrictions on gender. In Margaret Thatcher's heyday the blame for the moral ills of society was laid firmly at the feet of the family. As this novel reminds us, it was the family's moral obligation to take responsibility for those of its members who fell foul of social mores, and to ensure that 'care in the community' worked. The family has long been one of the most morally charged arenas for political debate in society. Michele Barrett contends:

> The tendency of the family-household is to encourage conservatism and militate against protest, and the close relationship between the economic aspect of the household and highly intense

personal and emotional relationships is an important factor in this ... [The family] has proved a stable ... system both for the reproduction of labour power, and as an arrangement to contain personal life, in the face of major social upheavals.[13]

The Fanshawe family is *almost* contained after the murder: the First World War takes the life of the elder son and the whole tragic story becomes the stuff of melodrama, its impact militated by the economic surety of the family and its social status. Only the apparition of the girl breaks through the surface veneer that closes back over the family. Simultaneously, Nick loses a physical foothold in the past when his grandfather dies. Geordie's death is a huge upheaval for Nick, 'like the side of the house going' (*AW* 249), the metaphor returning us to the fragile foundations of the family home.

Much of the novel's emotional impact reflects the point of view of its most ruminative character, Nick, who searches for meaning as he dedicates himself to his grandfather in his dying days. Geordie is Nick's mirror, in which he sees himself reflected as son and grandson while trying to knit those roles with father and husband. His struggle is to connect the members of his family, who are divided into two discrete units; only at Geordie's funeral do most of them come together. More generally he struggles to connect one time – his own – with another – that of his grandfather and the Fanshawes. The twisted gargoyles of the Fanshawes on his living-room wall, and the dragon's teeth and concrete bunkers at the beach left over from the war, may be disturbing reminders of the past, but fear of the future dominates now Nick has become the 'older generation'. Nick finds he is unable to interpret one world without recourse to another. Bertolt Brecht has argued that we should allow each epoch its heterogeneity and its elasticity: 'We must leave them their distinguishing marks and keep their impermanence always before our eyes so that our own period can be seen to be impermanent too.'[14] In *Another World*, Barker, like Brecht and Brodsky, unfixes the order of things so that ideas that refuse to fit neatly into a packaged past are left to haunt the reader at the end of the novel.

7

Understanding not Condemning: *Border Crossing*

> The monument of psychoanalysis must be traversed – not bypassed.
>
> (Roland Barthes, *Camera Lucida*, 1980)

THE DEATH OF SAFETY

Hidden in Barker's first novel, *Union Street*, is a desperate cameo of Mrs Biggs of Wharfe Street:

> She'd kept herself to herself. She was a clean-living, even religious woman, respected, if not much liked. Then her son, who was a bit not-all-there, had molested and strangled a little boy and left his body on a rubbish tip. Then nothing that Mrs Biggs could say or do would save her. On the night before they hanged her son, somebody had gone and smeared dogshit all over her windows and all over her front door. And they'd gone on doing it too. They never let up. She went loony in the end and had to be taken away. (*US* 186)

Also in Barker's first novel, a minor character, Laura, is diagnosed as schizophrenic ('She's living in a different world. So *they* say') and sets fire to an old man because he is of 'no use' (*US* 179). Barker studs her novels with such disturbing incidents. In the same novel, young Richard Scaife reacts to his father's death by developing a fascination with fire: 'On the night of his father's funeral ... [his mother] had come downstairs to find a fire blazing halfway up the chimney and Richard crouched over it, throwing handfuls of salt into the

94

flames' (*US* 171). Much later Barker herself throws salt into the flames when, out of such images and incidents, she creates Danny Miller/Ian Wilkinson in *Border Crossing*, a murderous child.

There have been other murderous children: in *Another World* Gareth begins by skimming pebbles at his baby half-brother but is soon throwing stones, endangering the life of the child. In a related storyline in the same novel, a brother and sister conspire to murder their baby brother and are acquitted because it seems inconceivable to a courtroom of adults that two privileged children could commit such a heinous act for no reason. Barker's latest work is a psychological novel that turns on the study of evil and, more unsettling still, our complicity with evil, on what Blake Morrison watching the trial of Robert Thompson and Jon Venables called 'the unthinkable thought of, the undoable done'. But Morrison was in no doubt that judging the Bulger case was like 'trying to catch the wind in your hands' or trying to 'iron out the creases from the sea'.[1] Evil is a subject many of us tend to distance ourselves from, since the presence of evil reminds us that the veneer of civilization is dangerously thin.

As in *Another World*, the characters in *Border Crossing* continue to live in the 'shadow of monstrosities', specifically young Danny Miller's murder of Lizzie Parkes, an old lady of 76 who in her dying moments struggles against an apparently motiveless child attacker. It is Danny's relationship with the psychologist who acted as the expert witness at his trial that dominates *Border Crossing*. Tom Seymour's marriage is collapsing. His and Lauren's relationship is as derelict and untended as the environment in which they live. The old Newcastle docks close to their home seem a kind of No Man's Land across which invisible emotional boundaries have been erected; they walk through them side by side, but Lauren is already spending most of her time in London. Tom is vulnerable and empty on a number of fronts. He is trying to finish a book against a deadline, and still grieving for the father he lost two years previously, when a grown-up Danny re-enters his life as 'Ian Wilkinson' one cold day. Danny uses unusual means to persuade the psychologist to initiate a series of sessions designed to help him come to terms with the evil in his past. But Danny is not all he seems. Social worker and friend Martha acts as the voice of reason when she warns Tom, 'you don't want an empty space at the centre of your life when you've got somebody like Danny prowling round the edges' (BC 172). The novel becomes a study of what happens when one person grafts his life on to another's and the usual depersonalization of evil that takes place in contemporary society is undermined.

Barker examines what we might term the death of safety in contemporary society, the kind of fear and sickness Andrew O'Hagan also describes in *The Missing* (1995), a book influenced by the James Bulger case. It has been reported that as many as thirty people stopped or watched Thompson and Venables as they walked with James Bulger to the railway line in Walton, a suburb of Liverpool, where the 2-year-old met his death. People questioned them but passed on. Barker raises the question of what happens when society begins to fear children. Adolescents, like Zit and Whitey's gang in *Liza's England*, have long been the focus of moral panics, but small children have been a cause for real social concern much more rarely. John Major's infamous statement that 'we must condemn a little more, and understand a little less' reminds us of how anxious contemporary society has become. In *Border Crossing*, Tom's research into 'children who kill' as part of a Youth Violence Project draws the reader into an uncomfortable world in which the rational and moral can be overturned: 'Somewhere in the back of his mind ... was the picture of a rope, fraying, one strand after another coming apart' (BC 27). Michelle has bitten off the nose of her foster mother's natural daughter; Jason started a fire in which four people died; a group of small boys have thrown a security guard down an escalator in a shopping mall, and on and on. Siegfried Kracauer has argued that the detective novel shows a civilized society its own face in a purer (and therefore more disturbing) way than society is usually accustomed to seeing it.[2] It is an interesting assertion that I would extend to the psychological thriller as deployed by Barker in *Blow Your House Down, The Eye in the Door*, and most disturbingly *Border Crossing*.

STARING ONE'S THERAPEUTIC METHOD IN THE FACE

In Robert Louis Stevenson's *The Strange Case of Doctor Jeckyll and Mr Hyde* (1886) and Barker's *The Eye in the Door* the split personality separates the social and ethical from the sexual and sinful. Barker is clearly fascinated by popular nineteenth-century ideas of evil and by the development of the psychological sciences in the twentieth century. The idea that 'man is not truly one, but truly two',[3] which Karl Miller famously discusses in *Doubles: Studies in Literary History* (1985), clearly underpins her representation of the therapeutic process, and the dominance of images of the skull or the head across the novels extends Kracauer's image of society's disturbing face. Barker recalls being struck by a very specific image of the human face:

> The specimen of a human head that my husband had when training was of a very beautiful young man with just faint spikes under the skin where his beard had grown after death. The other side of the face had been flayed to expose the organs. So you could walk around the figure to see youth and beauty and what lay beneath. It was a Victorian grotesque piece. (AI)

Barker had wondered whether Rivers in staring at such a head would 'stare at his therapeutic method and the scientific method of the anthropologist straight in the face' (AI). When the analogy is extended to Danny in *Border Crossing*, one remembers that at their first session Tom is aware that his patient is a fissured subject. He senses the presence of 'that child, immured inside the man' (*BC* 49) and notes how carefully Danny controls his facial expression throughout what proves to be a shaky procedure.[4] The encounter takes place in a perplexing borderland in which Tom does not see Danny clearly. Whenever he begins to approach the core of the boy's psychological problems, he pulls back: the guilt he feels about his role of expert witness at the boy's trial exacerbates the need to shield the boy. He becomes protective each time the young man appears to confide in him so that, when Danny confides that he would have liked to rip a prison governor to shreds, Tom is anxious that he should not speak in such violent terms to others.

Barker is interested in therapy but refuses to represent it as a panacea for society's ills. Rather, the social pathologies in which we discover the seeds of evil acts are scrutinized, alongside psychotherapy – or 'the talking cure' – as a methodology. Barker continues her exploration of the analytical processes Rivers and Prior, and Helen and Geordie engage in. She pursues the 'talking cure' in still more analytical detail in *Border Crossing*. Of Geordie in *Another World* she has said, 'I think one of the definitions of being creative is the amount of disturbing material you can permit into your life before you start to panic. With Geordie it is an enormous amount' (AI). In *Border Crossing* that creativity shifts into much more disquieting territory. Through Danny Miller, Barker sustains her most stringent critique to date of psychological convention and context. Elaine Showalter fears that we have 'too often overlooked metaphor, convention, context and intertextuality . . . The hysterical narration of fiction can tell us a lot more about the causes and cures of hysteria than most of the self-help books on the market.'[5] When James Bulger was murdered by two 10-year-old boys in 1993, newspapers turned to those for whom the imagination and its dramatization are a profession. The press turned to novelists like William Golding, author of *The Lord of the Flies*, Martin Amis, and Blake Morrison to provide context and intertextuality, to editorialize and to judge. Fiction is often the forum in which taboos, or topics to which it is just easier to turn a blind eye, are first explored, and Barker is just the writer to light the touchflame.

Instead of translating the hysterical narrative into a significant and coherent pattern for the reader, Barker recognizes the universal human need to create such patterns and undermines it. She unsettles the reader, allowing the causes and cures to remain ambivalent, while pursuing the ways in which they impact on each of us. One character comments derisively during a serious conversation about helping Danny to come to terms with his past, 'It amuses me sometimes to think about the talking cure, and how it's become a whole bloody industry, and how little evidence there is that it does a scrap of good' (*BC* 130). He is told by a psychologist, Tom, that there is indeed some evidence to suggest that counselling may be harmful to those who suffer a traumatic event because the process of recovery should involve an inevitable period of numbness that should not be disturbed or displaced. Rather than flatten that process into a dramatic plotline, Barker shows that therapy as conversation is too restricting when subjectivity exists in language. It is impossible to differentiate between what Danny remembers and the story 'Ian' tells about Danny. The child Danny supposedly feels angry about his mother's passivity in the face of a controlling husband whose physicality dominates the household: he hits his wife and humiliates his young son by hanging him up on a hook in the barn. Even his shaving is ritualistic; performed in the kitchen before the family, it serves as a prelude to a drunken violent evening. Danny displaces his anger at his father: his violent propensity is first played out on his mother. When she tries to strike him with the army belt his father had worn, he smashes her against a wall. Shortly afterwards he is killing Lizzie Parkes. Barker unpacks what is a neat and phased reaction to a bullying father and shows that Danny is more than the sum of his parts.

Whereas in *Another World* Geordie's words are authenticated by Helen's research and popular interest in veterans renders him a public spokesman for a generation, *Border Crossing*'s Danny Miller is set outside society from the age of 12 to 22. When the book opens he has been living in the world for some ten months under an assumed identity to protect him from media attention and extralegal activity on the part of vigi-lantes.[6] He is living life in the interstices of a fragile present, hiding his past from others while apparently seeking it out for himself. But his account of himself is problematized, not only in the story he tells but because of the way Danny orchestrates how people respond to him. He has a disarmingly charming exterior. At Long Garth, a secure unit, he is instrumental in ensuring that four teachers leave their jobs; he manipulates their attention and pushes them into a position where their professionalism is compromised in specific relation to their overinvolvement with him. In one case, that of a young gay teacher called Angus, Danny makes an accusation of sexual assault, something the teacher denies years later though does nothing to contest at the time. The metaphor Angus hits upon to describe what happened to him is telling: 'He cut my head off' (*BC* 159). In this novel the violence at its centre is all the more unnerving because it so often simmers in a metaphor. The conversation in which Angus admits this to Tom takes place in bucolic surroundings, on the Yorkshire moors. But peace is shattered by the desolate almost-human screaming of a rabbit caught in a trap. Behind the picturesque moors scene lies so much more, like the shadow of gruesome murders carried out by Myra Hindley and Ian Brady in the mid-1960s.

Some of the most disturbing scenes that Barker has created involve physical violence, like Kelly's rape in *Union Street* and Kath's murder in *Blow Your House Down*. Kath's rape and murder are presented dialogically – that is to say, the reader is compelled to view it from the point of view of the murderer as well as that of his victim. Elderly Liza in Barker's third novel is left for dead by a gang of youths. Her powerlessness in the face of their violence is difficult to witness. Barker goes into detail in the earlier novel, rendering the exchange between the old lady and her attackers in brutal clarity. The boys punch Liza and threaten to kill her pet parrot: 'Tell us where it is or I'll wring his fucking neck.' But her point of view still dominates:

> 'She's dead. You've killed her, you stupid cunt.'
> A scuffle, a flail of fists and feet, as they fought each other to get out. Then, silence.
> They were wrong, she decided after a while. He hadn't killed her, though there was a taste in her mouth that she recognized as blood. (*LE* 268–9)

However, in *Border Crossing* the crucial violent event at the centre of the novel remains enigmatic. Danny's point of view dominates; Lizzie is contained within his narrative of events and the reader is not allowed access to her interior world. The reader comes to understand that Danny kicked the old lady down her stairs and suffocated her with a pillow. Forensic evidence also shows that he 'played with her' after death and wrenched her rings off bruised fingers. Danny seems to return to the central violent incident of this life in his sessions with Tom, but he is a liar who suffers from what the reader understands as a borderline personality disorder and Tom has far more invested in his client than the reader deems wise. The horrific act that Danny commits is not described. In a period

when television and film provide so many graphic representations of murder, Barker shows that to confront the act by
representing it is not to confront its underlying menace or
larger social meaning.[7]

THERAPY AS CONVERSATION

One facet of Barker's critique is of the media and TV talk show
culture as part of a therapy-happy society in which media
buzzwords function like 'self-help' manuals.[8] Tom becomes a
personality, an expert witness on a TV show that, on the one
hand, presses for more public discussion of issues like the right
to privacy for criminals who have served their time, but, on the
other, fires up public opinion and does little to counter
ignorance. It is the media machine that precipitates the end of
Tom's sessions with Danny when the paparazzi seek the boy
out and he is forced to flee. Even the creative writing course
Tom sits on the edge of while waiting to interview Danny's
teacher has caught the therapy bug. One tutor's comments
have split two elderly sisters by forcing them to talk about a
father they remember in totally opposite ways. They are
broken by the experience and cannot be reconciled, but the
tutor believes that it is his job to find 'the grit in the oyster' in
order to develop their writing 'voice'. Another teacher is
scathing about the amateur writers taking part: they are
'hardly the Katherine Mansfield and Virginia Woolf *de nos
jours*' (*BC* 150). A visiting writer is atrociously monotone and
the audience falls asleep, belching and farting after too much
wine and cheese. Barker refuses to subscribe to any packaged
formulas.

She ensures that Danny cannot simply be read according to
a behaviourist model, whereby his anti-social behaviour is
explained away as a result of social circumstances. In fact, Tom
allows that 'The main pitfall in assessing the mental state of an
offender is to produce a report that fits the crime, rather than
the symptoms of the particular individual who is alleged to
have committed it' (*BC* 19). Tom falls foul of the very axiomatic
statements that shape his life as a psychologist. Danny's home
life is fractured, but his rural upbringing in a community

where everyone knows everyone else ensures that his crime should not be easily equated with social deprivation, or urban decay, or 'stranger-danger'. A therapeutic model risks de-emphasizing the individual's responsibility for playing out power games, disguising them as the product of Danny's circumstances. Tom searches for the root of Danny's pathology in the conditions of his childhood but the young man responds in a language of rational expectations. He presents a picture of his father that falls into a sociologist's understanding of 'compulsory masculinity', intermeshing violence with virility and authority. The father bulks large in Danny's childhood despite his absences; he is fascinated by his apparent strength: 'He was tall, he was strong . . . he had a gun . . . he could do no wrong.' Where the father is emotionally disabled in his relations with others, Ian is incredibly literate, so much so that he confounds the patterns that Tom has come to recognize through his research. He analyses his past for Tom, presenting it to him in consumer-friendly form: 'He hit me to get at her' (BC 137) and 'I hated her because I couldn't help her' (BC 139).

Danny describes for Tom how his allegiance changes from mother to father, fitting closely with a Freudian framework of analysis. Tom hears Danny slip into a voice that seems more his father's than his own, moving in and out of present and past tenses, and setting up doubt in Tom's mind as to whether he was right in his early assessment of the boy. Barker allows that Danny carefully breaks down the component parts of Tom's analysis.[9] He creates Freudian 'leads' for his therapist, controlling each component of the story he tells and even describing a psychotic break that occurred when he set fire to his bedroom as a child. He provides a pseudo-objective commentary in which children like him become generic, describing himself feeling alienated, 'you know, exiled – the way kids do when they're in bed and everything's still going on downstairs' (BC 88).

Danny is articulate, if edgy, and ironic. He even asks his own therapist about his feelings:

> Danny leaned forward. 'Can I ask you what you think – no, sorry, what you *feel* – about the trial?'
> 'What I feel? I'm not sure my feelings are relevant.'

'Oh, I think they are.'

Tom's mind flooded with images of the courtroom. The small, lonely figure in the dock. 'Uneasy,' he said at last.   (*BC* 58)

His account is a story-within-a-story constructed for Tom. It falls self-consciously outside the confessional. As a university student of Literature, Danny is more aware than most of how narratives function. When he talks about his teacher Angus supposedly abusing him, he adds, 'It was all so bloody repressed you wouldn't believe. Talk about Jane Austen' (*BC* 138) and allows that, at school, he 'got addicted to the . . . intensity' of writing about his past.

Barker lets Danny push at the boundaries of psychoanalytical explanation until his character seems to disintegrate or collapse in on itself. Danny's disassociation in the later stages of the therapeutic process is reminiscent of Prior's hysterical fugues in *The Eye in the Door*. Discussing Billy Prior, Barker has said that what makes him so difficult as Rivers's subject is his 'almost parasitic ability to weave his way between the cracks' in his analyst's mind (AI). Prior bitingly accuses Rivers of acting like a piece of 'empathic wallpaper', a metaphor to which Barker returns in exposing Danny for whom any therapeutic conversation is necessarily an amalgam of at least two personalities, the analyst's and the analysand's, even before one considers the splits in Danny's own character. In the process of engaging with Danny, Tom loses his 'value detachment' – the 'splinter of ice' the psychologist needs to remain self-consciously objective melts (*BC* 10). By the end of their very first session, Tom is completing his patient's sentences for him and Danny's postural congruence is an early sign – the 'almost synchronous mirroring' of the man by the boy (*BC* 32) – that Danny borrows his moods and behaviour from others. He freely admits, 'I don't always manage to distinguish between what I'm feeling and what other people are feeling. I seem to be . . .'. He pauses and Tom quickly supplies a suitable adjective: 'Permeable' (*BC* 59). Tom fails to heed the warnings of others, especially when their advice conflicts with his protection of Danny.

The ambiguous sexual charge of the wryly flirtatious Billy Prior becomes a much more threatening form of manipulation on Danny's part. He penetrates Tom and uncannily seems to know how his mind works: 'I'm like you, Tom, I remember voices. I remember the way people move, but you've got to remember there really are people who never forget a face' (*BC* 165). Danny has never forgotten Tom's face and he has stalked him. He has clearly read the transcript of his own trial yet presents it as 'memory'; his return is a 'systematic rebuttal' (*BC* 191) of the evidence Tom supplied at the trial and, consequently, also a form of denial of responsibility, no matter what he may say in therapy. He has elaborately constructed a retelling of events whereby the man (Ian) exonerates the boy (Danny).

Throughout the novel there are pauses in the therapeutic conversation that Tom and Danny try to have. Tom 'lets a silence open up' and both participants 'let the silence re-create the space around them' (*BC* 177). Silence is an important marker of what is not said, as I discussed in my Introduction to this study and in regard to *Liza's England*. In *Border Crossing*, when Tom tells the courtroom at Danny's trial that the boy has no difficulty in distinguishing between good and evil, a sigh ruffles the room like a sharp intake of breath. No words are spoken, but, when the audience in the courtroom sighs into the silence, it becomes clear that Tom's testimony changes the way that the jury thinks about the boy. Silence is especially complex in the psychotherapeutic context that Barker creates in this novel. One psychologist, Heidi M. Levitt, has identified seven different kinds of pause in a therapeutic conversation: disengaged pauses, emotional pauses, interactional pauses, reflexive pauses, expressive pauses, associational pauses, and mnemonic pauses. If Freud typically viewed silence as obstructive resistance on the part of the individual under analysis, Barker, like Levitt in 'Sounds of Silence', challenges the idea that silences are homogenous, that they always mean the same thing. Pauses can be 'active moments' and may even signal the therapist's anxiety or intimacy with the client.[10] It is the meaning beyond words that creates the disturbing undercurrent in *Border Crossing*. Tom finds his life taken up by Danny even in the spaces between their conversations; Danny may suffer from a 'borderline' personality, but it is Tom who crosses the professional border in his dealings with the young man.

CROSSING BORDERS

Even in the final chapter, in many ways an epilogue, that finds Tom and Martha embarking on a romantic relationship after the break-up of his marriage, there is an unrelieved sense of disquiet. Tom has witnessed a distraught Danny's psychotic break, a moment in which fascination with fire overwhelmed his ability to think about safety or behave rationally. Danny has proved he can still be a danger to himself and others. Yet Tom remains silent and does not expose him. His silence is protective but it also feeds the fear that there are hidden depths that remain dangerous waters for Danny to charter. Beyond 'Ian Wilkinson', the adult Danny's fragile identity, there is a new incarnation, a student visibly at ease with his peers in a new town. Tom says this 'new' Danny is a success, 'precarious, shadowed, ambiguous, but worth having nevertheless', but the smell of lilacs overwhelms him as he stares after the young man, and we are reminded of the famous opening to T. S. Eliot's *The Wasteland*:

> April is the cruellest month, breeding
> Lilacs out of the dead land, mixing
> Memory and desire, stirring
> Dull roots with spring rain.

Danny may have been reincarnated out of a redundant identity, but Barker refuses to soothe the reader with uncomplicated homilies about social rehabilitation. Danny is neither entirely absolved by his own confession nor exonerated by his psychologist and his tendency to pyromania remains unresolved and repressed. One of his teachers says of Danny, 'I don't think we even scratched the surface' (*BC* 132), and the reader wonders whether by the end of the novel Tom has managed to do much more.

The sole exception to the disquiet produced by the borderline metaphor that runs throughout this novel would seem to be the rebuilding of Newcastle's docklands, the area around Tom's home: 'All around Tom's street, shops, restaurants and hotels were springing up. Even the river changed. The crumbling jetties and quays were demolished, paths laid, trees planted' (*BC* 213). Urban revival is after all a form of regeneration and Newcastle's historic quayside district was revitalized as part of the Newcastle Initiative Scheme of the 1990s, which selected inner-city sites for renewal. But, when one looks more closely, urban regeneration is also gentrification at the expense of poorer communities who do not share in a neighbourhood's new prosperity (one is reminded of Margaret Thatcher's vision of renewal, based in Victorian urban policies but without the commitment of those like Jesse Boot and Joseph Chamberlain to individual cities). Loft apartments and dockland townhouses are priced beyond the pockets of the indigenous population, as Barker points out in *Liza's England*. The novel closes with little to console the reader beyond the fragile hope that healthier new lives may grow out of old ones.

In *Border Crossing*, Danny is a complex character over which a plethora of speakers disagree. He is a site of enquiry through which Barker challenges the reader to explore the nature of evil. She explored this idea in *Blow Your House Down*. Maggie is stunned when she hears a neighbour gossiping that her husband was also her attacker:

> You thought evil was simple. No, more than that, you made it simple, you froze it into a single shape, the shape of a man waiting in the shadows. But it wasn't simple. This woman, this wheezy middle-aged woman, with her corrugated-iron hair and her glasses that flashed when she looked sideways to see how you were taking it, she knew what she was doing. And she was enjoying it. You couldn't put evil into a single, recognizable shape. (*BYHD* 147–8)

Hannah Arendt reporting on Rudolf Eichmann's trial for crimes against humanity judged him to be an unassuming, pedestrian little man. Barker contends in *Blow Your House Down* that the serial killer is a man among men *as well as* a social aberration. One of the most disturbing aspects of *Border Crossing* is precisely Danny's ordinariness. Barker reworks a signature scene for boys, a scene that provoked laughter in Barry Hines's classic tale of working-class childhood, *A Kestrel for a Knave* (1969), when Billy Casper's classmate Anderson tells the class about his feet squelching into wellington boots filled to the brim with tadpoles. His is an exciting, sensual, and lively tale that celebrates a boy's ability to tell it. In a different context, in *The Missing*, Andrew O'Hagan remembers self-critically how, aged 8, he and other children engaged in the 'dangerous thrill' of almost drowning a toddler. In *Border Crossing* Tom remembers such an incident in his otherwise uneventfully happy childhood – but very differently.

Tom passes the pond where he and Jeff Bridges played as boys and remembers how one particular day, out collecting frog spawn with Jeff's young brother Neil, a game went too far when the boys filled Neil's boots with frog spawn. Barker sets the scene as pastoral but the 'cruel joke' on Neil makes the boy wet himself in fright. A man passing by on a bus leaps off to rescue the toddler: 'Three children were saved that day. A man glances up from his newspaper, sees what's going on, acts on what he sees. Accident. A more interesting news story, a thicker coat of dirt on the bus window, a disinclination to intervene, and it might have ended differently. In tragedy, perhaps' (*BC* 48). Barker creates a moment of irony tinged with knowingness; Tom commits a cruel childish act despite the moral teaching of his family but he files it away so that 'the person' who did that 'was not sufficiently like his present self for him to feel guilt'. Everything comes back to Danny. Tom is like Danny. Danny is like so many other boys but he was not saved from himself and no one saved Lizzie Parkes from him. Tom cannot bring himself quite to acknowledge that he could have been Danny, but the reader is made uncomfortably aware of the 'near miss' that exists in so many childhood pasts.

In *Border Crossing* Barker asks how we assign meaning to violence when, on the one hand, it is all too familiar and pervasive and, on the other, it shocks and catches us unawares. The violence Danny commits seems childishly gratuitous. He gains so little, just a little money to waste on space invader games, but so much distress is created for the man whose childhood actions colour each aspect of his adult life. Violence can colonize our lives and imaginations and shows no signs of diminishing in either the real or the imaginary spheres.[11] One feeling that the reader takes away from this powerful novel is panic at one's inability to control one's life or one's surroundings.

8

Postscript

The title *Border Crossing* is an effective metaphor for under-standing one of the key features of Barker's œuvre. Barker is a writer who looks straight at her subject, but she is constantly engaging with ambiguities. In *Border Crossing*, Tom Seymour remembers in later years the day that he and his wife walked around the docklands near their home, talking about ending their marriage. However, he 'remembered what he couldn't possibly have seen: a gull's eye view of the path. A man and a woman struggling along . . . seeing in memory what in life he did not see, Tom freezes the frame' (*BC* 2). Barker's novels are narratives in which events are mediated by memory and imagination. They are never totalizing accounts. Most obvious-ly across the Trilogy Barker explores the confluence of history and fiction, purposefully interleaving one with the other in a way that animates the former and politicizes the latter. Barker's expertise in the field of economic and social history assures that she is aware of the uses of history in fiction, and of the work of materialist exponents like Georg Lukacs. Lukacs's *The Historical Novel* (1937), by foregrounding class struggle, fa-mously critiqued the popular historical novel's separation from mainstream literary fiction, and its emphasis on the individual at the expense of broader historical forces.[1] Barker's narrative techniques ensure that the mass destruction of the First World War is not lost to background and her poststructuralist intermeshing of the historical with the fictional ensures that imagined characters and historical figures originate out of the conditions of history. Barker makes history visible in novels as differently inflected as *Liza's England* and *Border Crossing*. She maps the contradictions of the age in her characters.

Barker's novels stand in trans-textual relation: allusions to previous texts occur and what I have called signature scenes coalesce to demonstrate her thematic concerns. Borders and boundaries are the primary sites of enquiry for Barker, whether she excavates life at the margins of society as in *Union Street* and *Blow Your House Down* or in the interstices between war and peace and between fiction and reality in *The Man Who Wasn't There*. Usually boundaries are found to be permeable membranes to 'another world': for Colin in *The Man Who Wasn't There* through his active imagination, for Nick and his family through their ghostly Victorian counterparts in *Another World*. In *Blow Your House Down*, the killer likes to envisage living on another dead planet and the ice age he imagines reflects the cold, hard, icy precision of the brutal murders he commits. In *Liza's England* both Liza and Stephen dream about the figures painted on Liza's box of memories on the night she dies. For Tom Seymour the boundary set between professional psychologist and patient is crossed and recrossed. Boundaries are untenable and borders are broken between worlds. In Barker's context, compulsory heterosexuality proves time and again that it is never a secure stronghold: from Colin's teenage sexual ambivalence to Prior's bisexual opportunism. Prior has been described by his creator as 'neither fish nor fowl nor good red herring' and his character, more than any other, comes to epitomize the disruptive 'double-take' that distinguishes Barker's œuvre to date.[2]

Rivers's disquisition on the importance of 'fathering', which like 'mothering' can take place *outside* familial territory, begins to destabilize the traditional equation between maternal care and nurturing long before the 'New Man' became a buzzword: 'He distrusted the implication that nurturing, even when done by a man, remains female, as if the ability were in some way borrowed, or even stolen, from women ... If that were true, then there was really very little hope' (*R.* 107). Sassoon, Owen, and Prior each feels a paternal responsibility for the 'boys' at the front; their 'fathering' subverts any cross-generational understanding of the term while maintaining its domesticity in a context very far from home. Barker reorients gender boundaries in a very specific discourse of masculine maternalism and draws the reader's attention to the paradoxes her characters discover in war and at the heart of family life. Prior adjudges at one point that 'Murder was only killing in the wrong place' and that killing someone is not necessarily the 'worst thing' (*GR* 44). Violence, patriotism, and moral surety each undergo a vigorous shaking across Barker's œuvre, as does society's typically flustered response to evil.

However, at the edge of tragedy, Barker finds humour, usually in those places where social mores are broken. In *The Ghost Road* there is a scene of vaudevillian, farcical comedy when Prior and Sarah scrabbling to dress after sex in her mother's living room, find the family have returned from church. Prior catches sight of Sarah's 'drawers', which were 'thrown across the family Bible, one raised leg drawing a decent veil over Job and his boils'. He snatches the knickers up and sits back with the Bible covering his unbuttoned flies. While Ada is in the kitchen, Sarah calmly steps into the drawers Prior tosses to her before her mother returns with the singularly ironic comment, 'You missed a good show' (*GR* 82–3). Candid and thought-provoking, daring and willing to take risks with character and context, Barker refuses to ride her moralism like a hobbyhorse. In fact, in *Another World* Nick asks why we look to the past at all and decides that it is to be 'humbled by the weight of human experience' rather than to learn anything (*AW* 73). Barker is courageous, wry, and never less than interrogative about each and every idea she places before us. She can be iconoclastic, breaking open taboo topics and opening out debates. Her novels have touched emotional chords for many readers from school age to old age.

Notes

CHAPTER 1. INTRODUCTION

1. See Sharon Monteith, 'Warring Fictions: Reading Pat Barker', *Moderna Sprak*, 91/2 (1997), 124–9.
2. See *Granta 3: The End of the English Novel* (1980).
3. Annabel Davis-Goff, 'War Shocks: *Regeneration*', *Entertainment Weekly*, 17 Apr. 1992, 52; Candice Rodd, 'A Stomach for War', *Independent on Sunday*, 12 Sept. 1993, 28–9; Philip Hensher, *Guardian*, 26 Nov. 1993.
4. Donna Perry, 'Pat Barker', in *Backtalk: Women Writers Speak Out* (New Brunswick, NJ: Rutgers University Press, 1993), 51.
5. Donna Perry, 'Going Home Again: An Interview with Pat Barker', *Literary Review*, 34/2 (Winter 1991), 237.
6. Barker quoted in Francis Spufford, 'Exploding Old Myths', *Guardian*, 9 Nov. 1995, 2–4. For a full discussion of Martin Ritt's twenty-six films, see Gabriel Miller, *The Films of Martin Ritt: Fanfare for the Common Man* (Jackson, Miss.: University Press of Mississippi, 2000).
7. Writers who extrapolate on class consciousness in this context, from Barker herself to James Kelman and Livi Michael, have each noted that readers and reviewers typically prefer *not* to be made to think about how society works in the fictions they read. See e.g. Sharon Monteith and Pat Wheeler, 'An Interview with Livi Michael', *Critical Survey*, 12/3 (2000), 94–107.
8. For an elucidatory discussion of the ways in which the working classes have been represented in fiction and for 'an expanded lexicon of labor in cultural critique', see Peter Hitchcock, 'They Must Be Represented? Problems in Theories of Working-Class Representation', *PMLA* 115 (Jan. 2000), 20–32.
9. Eric Hobsbawm, 'The Age of Total War', in *Age of Extremes: The Short Twentieth Century 1914–1991* (London: Michael Joseph, 1994), 21–53.

10. In *Language, Counter-Memory, Practice: Selected Essays and Interviews*, ed. and intro. Donald Bouchard (Ithaca, NY: Cornell University Press, 1984), Foucault explains that official or traditional history 'aims at dissolving the singular event into an ideal continuity', whereas 'effective' history 'deals with events in terms of their most unique characteristics, their most acute manifestations' (p. 154). What interests Foucault is the 'progression of entangled events' because we exist among 'countless lost events, without a landmark or a point of reference' (p. 155). Or, as Hayden White describes in *The Content of Form: Narrative Discourse and Historical Representation* (Baltimore: Johns Hopkins University Press, 1987): 'Every narrative, however seemingly "full", is constructed on the basis of a set of events that might have been included but were left out; this is as true of imaginary narratives as it is of realistic ones' (p. 10).

11. Penny Smith, 'Remembered Poverty: The North-East of England', in Ian A. Bell (ed.), *Peripheral Visions: Images of Nationhood in Contemporary British Fiction* (Cardiff: University of Wales Press, 1995), 115.

12. Albert Einstein's aphorisms are published in Banesh Hoffman and Helen Dukas, *Albert Einstein, Creator and Rebel* (New York: Viking, 1972).

13. Pat Barker, 'Open Book', Radio 4, 26 Mar. 2001.

14. Dennis Brown, *The Modernist Self in Twentieth-Century English Literature* (London: Macmillan, 1989), 47–8.

15. Nicole Ward Jouve, *The Streetcleaner: The Yorkshire Ripper Case on Trial* (London: Marion Boyars, 1986), 144.

CHAPTER 2. STORIES OF 'THE OTHER BRITAIN': *UNION STREET* AND *BLOW YOUR HOUSE DOWN*

1. Michael I. Bochenski, *Theology from Three Worlds* (Macon, Ga.: Smyth & Helways, 1997), 70.

2. Elaine Showalter, *A Literature of their Own* (London: Virago, 1977), 314.

3. The Fawcett Prize is named after the suffragist Dame Millicent Fawcett. The novel was also runner-up for the *Guardian* Fiction Prize.

4. Raymond Williams, 'Structures of Feeling', in *Marxism and Literature* (Oxford: Oxford University Press, 1977), 128–35.

5. D. J. Taylor, *A Vain Conceit: British Fiction in the 1980s* (London: Bloomsbury, 1989), 127; Anne Boston, quoted in 'Pat Barker', *Contemporary Authors*, 122 (1988), 40.

6. Peter Hitchcock, 'Radical Writing', in *Dialogics of the Oppressed* (Minneapolis: University of Minnesota Press, 1993), 55.

7. See Iris Marion Young, 'The Ideal of Community and the Politics of Difference', in Linda J. Nicholson (ed.), *Feminism/Postmodernism* (New York: Routledge, 1990), 300; Simone de Beauvoir, *The Second Sex* (1949; London: Penguin, 1979), 508–16; Nina Auerbach, *Communities of Women: An Idea in Fiction* (Cambridge, Mass.: Harvard University Press, 1978). For a full discussion and critique of models of sisterhood and female community, see Sharon Monteith, *Advancing Sisterhood: Interracial Friendships in Contemporary Southern Fiction* (Athens, Ga.: University of Georgia Press, 2000).

8. George Orwell, *The Road to Wigan Pier* (London: Penguin, 1970), 6–11, 16–17.

9. Orwell's gender blindness has been discussed in detail by Beatrix Campbell in *Wigan Pier Revisited: Poverty and Politics in the Eighties* (London: Virago, 1984). It is worth noting that her book was published in the year of *Blow Your House Down*. See also John Kirk, 'Recovered Perspectives: Gender, Class and Memory in Pat Barker's Writing', *Contemporary Literature*, 40/4 (Winter 1999), 603–26. Kirk believes Barker is nostalgic and unpacks what that might mean in the history of cultural production with reference to Barker's first three novels. Raymond Williams could be similarly charged with failing to adumbrate women into his fiction. For a critique of Williams in this regard, see Jane Miller, 'The Great Silent Area', in *Seductions: Studies in Reading and Culture* (London: Virago, 1992).

10. Ian Haywood reads the novel very differently, stating that 'it is difficult to locate the action precisely or to locate the influence of regionalism on the lives of these women'. See 'Post-Industrial Fictions', in *Working-Class Fiction from Chartism to Trainspotting* (Plymouth: Northcote House, 1997), 145.

11. Ibid. 147.

12. Barker chose *Liza's England* but waited until the novel's republication in 1996 as a Virago Modern Classic to revert to her original title.

13. Olive Smelt was interviewed most recently for 'The Ripper's Bitter Legacy', *Daily Mail*, 1 Feb. 1997. When critics from outside the UK fail to locate Maggie's significance in the text, one is reminded of how closely Barker reads contemporary Britain and how insightful she is about specific crimes and events. See e.g. Kathy Pollitt, 'Bait for a Killer', *New York Times*, 21 Oct. 1984, and Barker's interview in *Contemporary Authors*, 42.

14. See Judith Walkowitz, *City of Dreadful Delight: Narratives of Sexual Danger in Late Victorian London* (London: Virago, 1992), for how

media coverage of the Ripper murders of 1888 policed women's movements to encourage them back into the home. See also Kate Clarke's essay on the ways in which the tabloid newspaper the *Sun* represents crimes of sexual violence against women: 'The Linguistics of Blame', in Deborah Cameron (ed.), *The Feminist Critique of Language* (London: Routledge, 1998).

15. Clive Bloom, 'The Ripper Writing: A Cream of a Nightmare Dream', in *Cult Fiction: Popular Reading and Pulp Theory* (London: Macmillan, 1996), 159–77.

16. Barker refuses to sensationalize her characters or deploy them as symbols of social degradation. If one turns to autobiographical work like June Levine and Lyn Madden, *Lyn: A Story of a Prostitute* (Dublin: Attic Press, 1987), and Frederique Delacoste and Priscilla Alexander, *Sex Work: Writings by Women in the Sex Industry* (London: Virago, 1988), whether the context is the British Isles or the United States, women are similarly candid about their experiences with clients, the police, and their children.

17. Philip Dodd, 'Lowryscapes: Recent Writing about "the North" ', *Critical Quarterly*, 32/2 (Summer 1990), 17–28.

CHAPTER 3. 'YOU DON'T KILL TIME, TIME KILLS YOU': STORYTELLING AND *LIZA'S ENGLAND*

1. Lyn Pykett, '*The Century's Daughter*: Recent Women's Fiction and History', *Critical Quarterly*, 29/3 (Autumn 1987), 71–7.

2. Walter Benjamin, 'The Storyteller', *Illuminations* (London: Fontana, 1982), 93.

3. Iris Murdoch, 'Against Dryness: A Polemical Sketch', in *Existentialists and Mystics* (New York: Penguin, 1999). See also Martha Nussbaum on the relation between love and philosophy in *Love's Knowledge: Essays on Philosophy and Literature* (New York: Oxford University Press, 1990).

4. For an illuminating discussion of Lively and Barker, see Margaretta Jolly, 'After Feminism: Pat Barker, Penelope Lively and the Contemporary Novel', in Alistair Davies and Alan Sinfield (eds.), *British Culture of the Postwar: An Introduction to Literature and Society 1945–1999* (London: Routledge, 2000), 58–82.

5. Ibid. 78; Patricia Waugh, *Feminine Fictions: Revisiting the Postmodern* (London: Routledge, 1989), 3.

6. Peter Hitchcock, 'Radical Writing', in *Dialogics of the Oppressed* (Minneapolis: University of Minnesota Press, 1993), 55. For Bakhtin's definition of the chronotope, see M. M. Bakhtin, 'Forms

of Time and Chronotope in the Novel', in *The Dialogic Imagination*, trans. Michael Holquist and Caryl Emerson (Austin, Tex.: University of Texas Press, 1981).

7. Tony Harrison, *V. and Other Poems* (London: Farrar, Strauss & Giroux, 1990), 33.

8. Donna Perry, 'Going Home Again: An Interview with Pat Barker', *Literary Review*, 34/1 (1991), 242.

9. William Maxwell, 'Nearing Ninety', *New York Times Magazine* (1997), reproduced in Cynthia Ozick (ed.), *The Best American Essays 1998* (Boston: Houghlin Mifflin, 1998), 173–5.

10. For a historian's view of these developments, see Miriam Glucksman, *Women Assemble: Women Workers and the New Industries in Inter-War Britain* (London: Routledge, 1990).

11. Michael Ross, 'Acts of Revision: Lawrence as Intertext in the Novels of Pat Barker', *D. H. Lawrence Review*, 26/1–3 (1995), 51–63.

12. See Ian M. L. Hunter, 'An Exceptional Memory', in Ulric Neisser (ed.), *Memory Observed: Remembering in Natural Contexts* (New York: W. H. Freeman, 1982), 418–24.

13. See W. H. R. Rivers, 'On the Repression of War Experience', *Lancet*, 2 Feb. 1918, at http://www.sassoonery.demon.co.uk/lancetpaper.htm

14. See National Trust, *Stanley Spencer at Burghclere* (London: National Trust, 1991); Duncan Robinson, *Stanley Spencer* (Oxford: Oxford University Press, 1990), and Emily Brooks, 'A Life Less Ordinary', *National Trust Magazine*, 94 (Autumn 2001), 51–5. My especial thanks go to Sue and Tom Weitzel for drawing my attention to Stanley Spencer's paintings.

15. Jenny Newman, 'Souls and Arseholes: The Double Vision of *The Century's Daughter*', *Critical Survey*, 13/1 (2001), 18–36.

16. Fredric Jameson, 'Postmodernism, or the Cultural Logic of Late Capitalism', *New Left Review*, 146 (1984), 53–92.

CHAPTER 4. PERFORMING THE SELF: *THE MAN WHO WASN'T THERE*

1. Examples of the 'escaper' type occur in Richard Hoggart's grammar school boy, in the post-war classic exploration of popular and mass culture *The Uses of Literacy* (Harmondsworth: Pelican, 1957), and in novels by David Storey and poetry by Tony Harrison.

2. Italo Calvino, 'Levels of Reality in Literature', in *The Literature Machine* (London: Picador, 1989), 108.

3. For a detailed discussion of the ways in which cinema defines identity, see Jeffrey Richards, *Films and British National Identity: From Dickens to Dad's Army* (Manchester: Manchester University Press, 1997), esp. ch. 5, 'National Identity Post-War'.

4. See e.g. Constantin Stanislavski, *An Actor Prepares* (1926; London: Penguin, 1967).

5. See Joseph Bristow, 'Schoolboys', in *Empire Boys: Adventures in a Man's World* (London: Harper Collins, 1991), esp. 88–9. Although he studies the public-school system, Bristow points up the kinds of compulsively masculine ideas that underpin Colin's imaginative world.

6. See e.g. Gail Braydon and Penny Summerfield, *Out of the Cage: Women's Experiences in Two World Wars* (London: Pandora, 1987).

7. Herbert Mitgang, 'A Story in the Imagination of a Boy' (Review of *The Man Who Wasn't There*), *New York Times*, 8 Dec. 1990.

8. Barker, in Donna Perry, 'Going Home Again: An Interview with Pat Barker', *Literary Review*, 34/2 (Winter 1991), 239.

9. See Bruno Bettelheim, *The Uses of Enchantment* (New York: Knopf, 1976).

10. Hoggart, *The Uses of Literacy*, 296.

11. Richard Hoggart, *Between Two Worlds* (London: Aurum Press, 2001). This collection of essays by the important cultural critic, now in his eighties, includes a number of observations that resonate for those who read and enjoy Barker's fiction. Hoggart continues to value those writers who reach across the world of their own experience to draw in intelligent readers who enjoy argument about and engagement with the politics of literature.

CHAPTER 5. 'WE WILL REMEMBER THEM': THE REGENERATION TRILOGY

1. Although it may be a central tenet when reading Owen's work, as Claire M. Tylee points out, focusing Owen study on poems like 'Anthem for Doomed Youth' detracts from the vindictiveness of 'Apologia Pro Poemate Meo'. Or, as Barker has argued, the gallows humour that characterizes his editing of the *Hydra* while at Craiglockhart in 1917. For Tylee's discussion, see *The Great War and Women's Consciousness: Images of Militarism and Womanhood in Women's Writing, 1914–1964* (London: Macmillan, 1990), 256. There are many collections of Owen's poems and good web sites of his work: http://www.rjgeib.com/heroes/owen/owen-poetry

2. Pat Barker, in *On the Ghost Road*, BBC 2, 14 May 1996.

3. Robin Stummer, 'The War We Can't Let Go', *Guardian*, 7 Nov. 1998.

4. See e.g. Johns Hopkins University's Gulf War Study, which focuses on the symptoms and medical condition of veterans at http://www.med.jhu.edu/gws/

5. Elaine Showalter, 'Male Hysteria: W. H. R. Rivers and the Lessons of Shellshock', in *The Female Malady: Women, Madness and English Culture 1830–1980* (London: Virago, 1987), 187.

6. Paul Fussell, *The Great War and Modern Memory* (Oxford: Oxford University Press, 1975), 7, 30.

7. *Hydra*, 10, 1 Sept. 1917. See the contents of the issue at http://www.napier.ac.uk/depts/library/craigon/warpoets/hydra.

8. Canonical texts like *Journey's End, All Quiet on the Western Front, Goodbye To All That*, and *Memoirs of an Infantry Officer* can act as a literary-historical lens through which to view Barker's contemporary exploration of the war at home, the anti-war effort in *The Eye in the Door*, and trench warfare.

9. Lyndall Gordon, *Virginia Woolf: A Writer's Life* (Oxford: Oxford University Press, 1968), 188.

10. See Felicity Goodall, *A Question of Conscience: Conscientious Objectors in the Two World Wars* (Stroud: Sutton, 1997).

11. See Michel Foucault, *Discipline and Punish: The Birth of the Prison* (1975; London: Penguin, 1991), for a detailed discussion of the Panopticon, and *Power/Knowledge: Selected Interviews and Other Writings 1972–1977* (New York: Pantheon, 1981), 155–6, for his discussion of the effects of self-policing.

12. Karin Westman, *Pat Barker's* Regeneration: *A Reader's Guide* (New York: Continuum, 2001), 44.

13. Barker, quoted in Anthony Quinn, 'What Sassoon Could Never Resolve', *Daily Telegraph*, 2 Sept. 1995.

14. Rivers's sister wrote a short memoir of Charles Dodgson (Lewis Carroll). See Katherine Rivers, *Memories of Lewis Caroll*, published with an introduction by Richard Slobodin for *McMaster University Library Research News*, 3 (1976).

15. Edith Bagnold, *Diary without Dates* (1918; London: Virago, 1978).

16. Seamus Heaney, *The Government of the Tongue* (London: Faber, 1988), p. xv; Niall Ferguson, *The Pity of War* (London: Allen Lane, 1998).

17. Jay Winter, *Sites of Memory, Sites of Mourning: The Great War in European Cultural History* (Cambridge: Cambridge University Press, 1997).

18. Blake Morrison, 'War Stories', *New Yorker*, 22 Jan. 1996, 78–80, 82.

19. Richard Slobodin first published his biography in 1976. The revised edition is endorsed by Barker in recognition of how her

fictional work has developed interest in Slobodin's subject. See *W. H. R. Rivers: Pioneer Anthropologist, Psychiatrist of* The Ghost Road (Stroud: Sutton, 1997).

20. Siegfried Sassoon, 'Letter to Robert Graves' (1918), in *Siegfried Sassoon: The War Poems*, ed. Rupert Hart-Davis (London: Faber, 1983), 119–22. In 1967 Sassoon published a new edition of *The Memoirs of George Sherston* in *Siegfried's Journey 1916–1920* (London: Faber, 1982), in which Owen appears in chapter 4.

21. See e.g. Anne M. Wyatt-Brown, 'Headhunters and Victims of the War: W. H. R. Rivers and Pat Barker', in Frederico Pereira, *Proceedings of the Thirteenth International Conference on Literature and Psychoanalysis* (Lisbon: Instituto Superior de Psicologia Aplicada, 1997), 53–9. Ben Shepherd studies the cult of facticity in 'Digging up the Past', *Times Literary Supplement*, 22 Mar. 1996, 12.

22. There are, of course, critics who precede Barker's retelling of Rivers, notably Elaine Showalter, whose important essay 'Male Hysteria' provides a full and discursive context for Barker's fictional extrapolation on the historical figure.

23. Tylee, *The Great War*, 257. For a full discussion of the lust for killing, see Joanna Bourke, *An Intimate History of Killing: Face-to-Face Killing in Twentieth-Century Warfare* (London: Granta, 1999), and Niall Ferguson, *The Pity of War* (London: Allen Lane, 1998).

24. Pat Barker discusses her views of the letters in *Kaleidoscope*, BBC Radio 4, 12 Sept. 1995. Owen's letters were collected by John Bell in 1967 and published in paperback.

25. Pat Barker, in Mark Sinker, 'Temporary Gentlemen and Pat Barker on the Film Adaptation of her Novel *Regeneration*', *Sight and Sound*, 12 (Dec. 1997), 24.

26. Robert Graves, 'The Morning before Battle', in James Reeves (ed.), *Georgian Poetry* (London: Penguin, 1962), 129. For a similar aesthetic sense, one might also consider R. H. Mottram, *The Spanish Farm* (1924), but the book has been out of print for a long time. Alain-Fournier was himself killed in action in France in 1914.

27. For example, in the *New Republic* (Stanley Kauffman on 14 Sept. 1998); the *National Review* (28 Sept. 1998); the *Minneapolis Star Tribune* (3 Oct. 1998). Most interestingly, despite the minor mistakes of fact in Jane Sumner's review, the *Dallas Morning News* declares *Regeneration* 'the best war picture of the year', deliberately comparing it with Spielberg's epic (28 Sept. 1998). For a recent discussion of the film, see Westman, *Pat Barker's* Regeneration, 69–72.

28. Scott is perhaps best known for the screenplay of Nicolas Roeg's classic *Don't Look Now* (1973), adapted from Daphne Du Maurier's short story.

29. W. B. Yeats, 'Introduction' to *The Oxford Book of English Verse* (Oxford: Oxford University Press, 1936), reprinted in J. Hollander (ed.), *Modern Poetry: Essays in Criticism* (Oxford: Oxford University Press, 1969), 83–104.

30. Westman, *Pat Barker's* Regeneration, 69.

CHAPTER 6. LOOKING FORWARD INTO THE PAST: *ANOTHER WORLD*

1. Suzie Mackenzie, 'Out of the Past', *Guardian*, 24 Oct. 1998, p. 31.

2. Roland Barthes, *Writing Degree Zero* (1953), trans. Annette Lavers and Colin Smith (New York: Hill & Wang, 1977), 46.

3. Around ten million soldiers perished during the First World War. The Commonwealth War Graves Commission (at www.cwgc.org) has overall responsibility for the care and maintenance of grave sites. For example, the France Area Office alone is responsible for 691,301 graves and 2,931 cemeteries as well as memorials to the missing, like the huge Menin Gate at Ypres, which is a monument to 54,896 soldiers who have no other resting place. Staff who tend to the sites, planting and pruning, and who repair the fabric of the graves and headstones, became the subject of news articles in 2000, when it was suggested that they were paid too little for such an important task.

4. Gilles Deleuze, *Cinema 2: The Time Image*, trans. Hugh Tomlinson and Robert Galeta (Minneapolis: University of Minnesota Press, 1989), 189.

5. Marita Sturken, *Tangled Memories* (Berkeley and Los Angeles: University of California Press, 1997), 74.

6. Pierre Macherey, *A Theory of Literary Production* (1966), trans. G. Wall (London: Routledge & Kegan Paul, 1978).

7. Walter Benjamin, 'The Storyteller', *Illuminations* (London: Fontana, 1992), 84.

8. Linda Grant, 'Violent Anxiety', in Sarah Dunant and Roy Porter (eds.), *The Age of Anxiety* (London: Virago, 1996), 23.

9. Sigmund Freud, 'Family Romances', in *On Sexuality: Three Essays on the Theory of Sexuality and Other Works* (Harmondsworth: Penguin, 1977), 221–5, at 221.

10. Christine Bridgewood, 'Family Romances: The Contemporary Popular Family Saga', in Jean Radford (ed.), *The Progress of*

Romance: The Politics of Popular Fiction (London: Routledge, 1997), 167–93.

11. Catherine Belsey, *Critical Practice* (London: Methuen, 1980), 78.

12. Michael Neve, 'Nuclear Fallout: Anxiety and the Family', in Dunant and Porter (eds.), *The Age of Anxiety*, 111.

13. Michele Barrett, *Women's Oppression Today* (London: Methuen, 1984), 212.

14. Bertolt Brecht, *Brecht on Theatre: The Development of an Aesthetic*, ed. and trans. John Willet (London: Methuen, 1964), 190.

CHAPTER 7. UNDERSTANDING NOT CONDEMNING: *BORDER CROSSING*

1. Blake Morrison, *As If* (London: Granta, 1997), 206.

2. Siegfried Kracauer, *The Mass Ornament: Weimar Essays*, ed. and trans. Thomas Y. Levin (Cambridge, Mass.: Harvard University Press, 1995).

3. See Karl Miller, *Doubles: Studies in Literary History* (Oxford: Oxford University Press, 1989).

4. For this reason I will refer to the character as Danny throughout, rather than his 'new' identity of Ian Wilkinson.

5. Elaine Showalter, *Hystories: Hysterical Epidemics and Modern Culture* (London: Picador, 1997), 99.

6. It was not until February 2001, when Barker's novel was already about to be published, that the controversy over the freeing of Thompson and Venables was aired across the media. Lord Wakeham, Chairman of the Press Commission, argued that granting the young men anonymity would be a dangerous precedent (a precedent Barker explores and exposes in fiction), whereas Dame Elizabeth Butler-Sloss, President of the Family Division of London's High Court who granted the order, maintained that they would be at serious risk otherwise. Mary Bell, who murdered two little boys in 1968, is the only person previously granted such an injunction. Like these characters, Danny is notorious and as such at the mercy of press and vigilantes.

7. For a wider discussion, see Martin Barker and Julian Petley (eds.), *Ill Effects: The Media/Violence Debate* (2nd edn.; London: Routledge, 2001).

8. For an analysis of talk shows and the ways in which women in particular respond to them, see Jane Shattuc, *The Talking Cure: TV Talk Shows and Women* (New York: Routledge, 1997).

9. 'Pat Barker in Conversation with Sharon Monteith', Hay on Wye Literary Festival, 2 June 2001.
10. Heidi M. Levitt, 'Sounds of Silence in Psychotherapy: The Categorization of Clients' Pauses', *Psychotherapy Research*, 11/3 (2001), 295–309. See also A. Sabbadini, 'Listening to Silence', *British Journal of Psychotherapy*, 7 (1991), 406–15.
11. Linda Grant wonders whether our anxious obsession with violence is a form of moral panic in 'Violent Anxiety', in Sarah Dunant and Roy Porter (eds.), *The Age of Anxiety* (London: Virago, 1996), 21. In a similar vein, Ann Scott discusses our violent fantasies in *Real Events Revisited* (London: Virago, 1996).

CHAPTER 8. POSTSCRIPT

1. Georg Lukacs, *The Historical Novel* (1937; Boston: Beacon Press, 1962).
2. Barker, in Jim Shepherd, 'Gentleman in the Trenches', *New York Times*, 15 May 1994.

Select Bibliography

WORKS BY PAT BARKER

Union Street (London: Virago, 1982).
Blow Your House Down (London: Virago, 1984).
The Century's Daughter (London: Virago, 1986); reissued as
    Liza's England (London: Virago, 1996)
The Man Who Wasn't There (London: Penguin, 1988).
Regeneration (London: Penguin, 1991).
The Eye in the Door (London: Viking, 1993).
The Ghost Road (London: Viking, 1995).
Another World (London: Viking, 1998).
Border Crossing (London: Viking 2001).
On the Ghost Road, BBC 2, 14 May 1996.

CRITICAL STUDIES

Books and Articles about Barker

Ardis, Ann, 'Political Attentiveness vs. Political Correctness: Teaching
    Pat Barker's *Blow Your House Down*', *College Literature*, 18/3 (Oct.
    1991), 44–54. Ardis's original approach combines literary criticism
    with a keen interest in pedagogy in exploring her predominantly
    middle-class American students' classroom responses to Barker's
    second novel.
Dodd, Kathryn, and Dodd, Philip, 'From the East End to *Eastenders*:
    Representations of the Working Class, 1890–1980', in Dominic
    Strinati and Stephen Wragg (eds.), *Come on Down?: Popular Media
    Culture in Post-War Britain* (London: Routledge, 1992), 116–32. This
    wide-ranging essay situates Barker's *Union Street* within a dis-
    cussion of soap opera and other dramatized forms in order to

compare representations of the working classes in popular cultural productions.

Harris, Greg, 'Compulsory Masculinity, Britain and the Great War: The Literary Historical Work of Pat Barker', *Critique: Studies in Contemporary Fiction*, 39/2 (June 1998), 290–304. Harris discusses the Trilogy with close reference to Siegfried Sassoon's writings in order to demonstrate the ways in which masculinity and hetero-sexuality were represented during the war years and to draw conclusions about Barker's creative interventions into the subject.

Hitchcock, Peter, 'Radical Writing', in *Dialogics of the Oppressed* (Minneapolis: University of Minnesota Press, 1993). The essay is also included in Dale M. Bauer and Susan Jaret McKinstry (eds.), *Feminism, Bakhtin and the Dialogic* (Albany, NY: State University of New York Press, 1991), 95–121. In this important essay Hitchcock reads Barker's early fiction through a critical lens that draws on Mikhail Bakhtin's theories of dialogism and heteroglossia in order to locate Barker firmly as a working-class writer.

Jolly, Margaretta, 'After Feminism: Pat Barker, Penelope Lively and the Contemporary Novel', in Alastair Davies and Alan Sinfield (eds.), *British Culture of the Postwar: An Introduction to Literature and Society 1945–1999* (London: Routledge, 2000), 58–82. Jolly's feminist approach involves a thought-provoking comparative study of two contemporary British novelists who might seem dissimilar initially but who draw on similar themes in their fiction.

Kirk, John, 'Recovered Perspectives: Gender, Class and Memory in Pat Barker's Writing', *Contemporary Literature*, 40/4 (Winter 1999), 603–26. This essay focuses on Barker's first three novels, *Union Street*, *Blow Your House Down*, and *Liza's England*. Kirk argues that Barker reworks images of working-class life in order to represent a community long hidden from history.

Lanone, Catherine, 'Scattering the Seed of Abraham: The Motif of Sacrificing in Pat Barker's *Regeneration* and *The Ghost Road*', *Literature and Theology*, 13/3 (Sept. 1999), 259–68. Lanone considers the ways in which *écriture feminine* and related ideas from French feminist thought may begin to open up ways of reading Barker's work.

Monteith, Sharon, 'Warring Fictions: Reading Pat Barker', *Moderna Sprak*, 91/2 (1997), 124–9. This essay discusses Barker's critical reception and argues that it is unhelpful to separate the writer's work on the basis of her explorations of female and male protagon-ists when similar preoccupations underpin the early work and the Trilogy.

Morrison, Blake, 'War Stories: What Booker Prize Winner Pat Barker Sees in Soldiers', *New Yorker*, 22 Jan. 1996, 78–80, 82. Morrison praises Barker's creative and critical exploration of war and warfare.

Newman, Jenny, 'Souls and Arseholes: The Double Vision of *The Century's Daughter*', *Critical Survey*, 13/1 (2001), 18–36. Newman provides a close reading of Barker's third novel, concentrating on Barker's exploration of silences and impeded communication.

Pykett, Lyn, '*The Century's Daughter*: Recent Women's Fiction and History', *Critical Quarterly*, 29/3 (Autumn 1987), 71–7. An important early critical response that situates Barker's novel in a discussion of women's writing and representations of history and memory.

Ross, Michael, 'Acts of Revision: Lawrence as Intertext in the Novels of Pat Barker', *D. H. Lawrence Review*, 26/1–3 (1995), 51–63. Ross takes Lawrence as his starting point for reading ritualistic working-class scenes in Barker's fiction.

Sinker, Mark, 'Temporary Gentlemen and Pat Barker on the Film Adaptation of her Novel *Regeneration*', *Sight and Sound*, 12 (Dec. 1997), 22–4. Sinker discusses the adaptation of *Regeneration* for the screen and talks to the author.

Westman, Karin, *Pat Barker's* Regeneration: *A Reader's Guide* (New York: Continuum 2001). This book provides an accessible introduction to the novel, a summary of the novel's reception, and a helpful list of discussion questions. It comprises a close reading of the novel with some attention also paid to Gillies MacKinnon's film adaptation of *Regeneration*.

Whitehead, Anne, 'Open to Suggestion: Hypnosis and History in Pat Barker's *Regeneration*', *Modern Fiction Studies*, 44/3 (Fall 1998), 674–94. This interesting essay explores ideas of therapy and memory. Whitehead argues that the act of remembering – or regenerating the past – inevitably involves characters (and by extension the narratives in which they figure) in a negotiation between a haunting past and an uneasy present.

Wotton, George, 'Writing from the Margins', in Ian A. Bell (ed.), *Peripheral Visions: Images of Nationhood in Contemporary British Fiction* (Cardiff: University of Wales Press, 1995). This essay locates Barker alongside other writers from the north-east of England, most particularly Jack Common, whose *Kiddar's Luck* was published in 1951. It focuses on issues of language and representation in the early work.

Wyatt-Brown, Anne M., 'Headhunters and Victims of the War: W. H. R. Rivers and Pat Barker', in Frederico Pereira (ed.), *Proceedings from the Thirteenth International Conference on Literature and Psychoanalysis* (Lisbon: Instituto Superior de Psicologia Aplicada, 1997), 53–9. This essay takes a psychoanalytic approach in its exploration of cross-generational relationships and cross-cultural communication focusing primarily on *The Ghost Road*.

Selected Interviews with Barker

Monteith, Sharon and Wheeler, Pat, 'Pat Barker', in Sharon Monteith, Jenny Newman, and Pat Wheeler (eds.), *Contemporary British Fiction: An Introduction through Interview* (London: Arnold, forthcoming). This interview includes discussion of *Border Crossing* and uses this book as the pivotal text through which to identify broad concerns across Barker's fiction.

Perry, Donna, 'Going Home Again: An Interview with Pat Barker', *Literary Review*, 34/2 (Winter 1991), 235–44. This interview concentrates in the main on *The Man Who Wasn't There* and the extent to which it may be read as autobiographical, though it also casts back to review earlier work.

——'Pat Barker', in *Backtalk: Women Writers Speak Out* (New Brunswick, NJ: Rutgers University Press, 1993), 43–61. This interview continues the conversation Perry began in 1991 and focuses on subjects like women's silences, expressions of anger, and aspects of Barker's own life that may be reflected in her fiction.

There are many more interviews on the World Wide Web and a number of sites focusing on Pat Barker and her work. For example:

http://www.mtmercy.edu/class/barker/bio.htm

http://www.nytimes.com.books/barker

http://www.ipl.org/cgi-bin/ref/litcrit/litcrit.out.re g-667

Contemporary British Fiction

Bell, Ian A. (ed.), *Peripheral Visions: Images of Nationhood in Contemporary British Fiction* (Cardiff: University of Wales Press, 1995).

Dodd, Philip, 'Lowryscapes: Recent Writing about "the North"', *Critical Quarterly*, 32/2: 17–28.

Gasiorek, André, *Post-War British Fiction: Realism and After* (London: Edward Arnold, 1995).

Haywood, Ian, *Working-Class Fiction from Chartism to Trainspotting* (Plymouth: Northcote House, 1997).

Hitchcock, Peter, 'They Must Be Represented? Problems in Theories of Working-Class Representation', *PMLA* 115 (Jan. 2000), 20–32.

Monteith, Sharon, 'Postmodernist Writing and Contemporary British Fiction: Are Contemporary British Novelists Writing about Contemporary Britain?' *Moderna Språk*, 92/1 (1998), 4–13.

Taylor, D. J., *A Vain Conceit: British Fiction in the 1980s* (London: Bloomsbury, 1989).

Todd, Richard, *Consuming Fictions: The Booker Prize and Fiction in Britain Today* (London: Bloomsbury, 1996).

Rivers, Sassoon, and Owen

Hibberd, Dominic, *Wilfred Owen: The Last Year* (London: Constable, 1992).

Hill, Susan, *Strange Meeting* (London: Penguin, 1973).

MacDonald, Stephen, *Not About Heroes: The Friendship of Siegfried Sassoon and Wilfred Owen* (London: Faber, 1983).

Moorcroft, Jean, *Siegfried Sassoon: The Making of a War Poet* (London: Gerald Duckworth, 1999).

Owen, Wilfred, *The War Poems*, ed. John Stallworthy (London: Chatto, 1994).

——*Selected Letters*, ed. John Bell (London: Oxford, 1998).

Roberts, John Stuart, *Siegfried Sassoon* (London: Metro, 2000).

Sassoon, Siegfried, *The War Poems*, ed. Rupert Hart-Davis (London: Faber, 1983).

——*Memoirs of an Infantry Officer* (London: Faber, 2000).

Showalter, Elaine, 'Male Hysteria: W. H. R. Rivers and the Lessons of Shellshock', in *The Female Malady: Women, Madness and English Culture 1830–1980* (London: Virago, 1987).

Slobodin, Richard, *W. H. R. Rivers: Pioneer Anthropologist, Psychiatrist of* The Ghost Road (Stroud: Sutton, 1997).

Stallworthy, John, *Wilfred Owen* (Oxford: Oxford University Press, 1988).

There are a number of good web sites on Craiglockhart and on Rivers, whose books and papers are not easily available, and several on Owen. For example:

http://www.sassoonery.demon.co.uk/lancetpaper.htm (includes Rivers, 'On the Repression of War Experience', *Lancet*, 2 Feb. 1918).

http://www.napier.ac.uk/depts/library/craigon/warpoets/hydra (includes *Hydra*, Craiglockhart Hospital newspaper).

http://www-instruct.nmu.edu/psychology/rivers (about Rivers).

http://www.rjgeib.com/heroes/owen/owen-poetry (about Owen's poetry).

War

Bourke, Joanne, *Dismembering the Male: Men's Bodies, Britain and the Great War* (London: Reaktion Books, 1999).

——*An Intimate History of Killing: Face-to-Face Killing in Twentieth-Century Warfare* (London: Granta, 1999).

——*The Second World War: A People's History* (Oxford: Oxford University Press, 2001).

Braydon, Gail, and Summerfield, Penny, *Out of the Cage: Women's Experiences in Two World Wars* (London: Pandora, 1987).

Commonwealth War Graves Commission at http://www.cwgc.org.

Faulks, Sebastian, and Hensgen, Jorg (eds.), *The Vintage Book of War Stories* (London: Vintage, 1999).

Ferguson, Niall, *The Pity of War* (London: Allen Lane, 1998).

Fussell, Paul, *The Great War and Modern Memory* (Oxford: Oxford University Press, 1975).

Glucksman, Miriam, *Women Assemble: Women Workers and the New Industries in Inter-War Britain* (London: Routledge, 1990).

Goodall, Felicity, *A Question of Conscience: Conscientious Objection in the Two World Wars* (Stroud: Sutton, 1997).

Hobsbawm, Eric, *Age of Extremes: The Short Twentieth Century 1914–1991* (London: Michael Joseph, 1994).

Keegan, John, *The First World War* (London: Hutchinson, 1998).

——(ed.), *The Penguin Book of War: Great Military Writings* (London: Penguin, 1999).

Mosse, George, *Fallen Soldiers: Reshaping the Memory of the World Wars* (New York: Oxford University Press, 1990).

Tylee, Claire M., *The Great War and Women's Consciousness: Images of Militarism and Womanhood in Women's Writing, 1914–1964* (London: Macmillan, 1990).

West, Rebecca, *The Return of the Soldier* (London: Virago, 1996).

Winter, Jay, *Sites of Memory, Sites of Mourning: The Great War in European Cultural History* (Cambridge: Cambridge University Press, 1997).

Woolf, Virginia, *Mrs Dalloway* (Harmondsworth: Penguin, 1996).

Contemporary Social Anxieties and Millennial Preoccupations

Barker, Martin, and Petley, Julian (eds.), *Ill Effects: The Media/Violence Debate* (2nd edn.; London: Routledge, 2001).

Delbanco, Andrew, *The Death of Satan: How Americans Have Lost the Sense of Evil* (New York: Noonday, 1996).

Dunant, Sarah, and Porter, Roy (eds.), *The Age of Anxiety* (London: Virago, 1996).

Showalter, Elaine, *Hystories: Hysterical Epidemics and Modern Culture* (London: Picador, 1997).

Morrison, Blake, *As If* (London: Granta, 1997).

Jouve, Nicole Ward, *The Streetcleaner: The Yorkshire Ripper Case on Trial* (London: Marion Boyars, 1986).

Scott, Ann, *Real Events Revisited* (London: Virago, 1996).

Shattuc, Jane, *The Talking Cure: TV Talk Shows and Women* (New York: Routledge, 1997).

Weeks, Jeffrey, *Sex, Politics and Society* (New York: Longman, 1981).

Index